African Parliamentary Reform

Some of the most far-reaching and innovative parliamentary reform is occurring in Africa. While these reforms are not yet widespread across the continent, parliaments in some African countries are asserting their independence as policymakers, as overseers of government and as the guardians of citizens' rights and needs.

This book presents recent reforms in selected African parliaments – Ghana, Kenya, Uganda, Tanzania, Rwanda, Benin, Zambia, Ethiopia, Liberia and Nigeria. It also presents cross-cutting innovations by African parliaments – in fighting corruption, in providing development to constituents and in combating climate change. Many of the chapters are authored by African MPs themselves, making this a book 'by MPs for MPs', as well as being of interest to students and scholars of African Politics, and to those international institutions that support parliamentary development.

African Parliamentary Reform is a joint initiative by the World Bank Institute, the Commonwealth Parliamentary Association and the Parliamentary Centre (Africa).

Rick Stapenhurst is a parliamentary consultant/advisor to the World Bank Institute, USA. His most recent publications include *Parliaments as Peacebuilders: The Role of Parliaments in Conflict Affected Countries*. **Rasheed Draman** is the Director of the Parliamentary Centre's program in Africa. His reports on African political developments include 'Poverty Reduction Strategy Process and Parliaments in Africa'. **Andrew Imlach** is the Director of Communications and Research at the Commonwealth Parliamentary Association Secretariat in London. Since 1983, he has been the Editor of *The Parliamentarian*, the Journal of Commonwealth Parliaments and Legislatures. **Alexander Hamilton** is a consultant at the World Bank Institute, USA, and is completing a PhD in political economy at the University of Oxford. **Cindy Kroon** currently works at the World Bank Institute specializing on the engagement of parliaments in the extractive industries sector. She previously worked at the Dutch Ministry of Foreign Affairs and the Dutch Central Bank.

Routledge research in comparative politics

African Parliamentary Reform

Edited by Rick Stapenhurst,
Rasheed Draman and Andrew Imlach
with Alexander Hamilton and
Cindy Kroon

Parliamentary Centre
le Centre parlementaire

CPA COMMONWEALTH
PARLIAMENTARY
ASSOCIATION

World Bank
Institute

Routledge
Taylor & Francis Group

LONDON AND NEW YORK

This edition published 2011
by Routledge
2 Park Square, Milton Park, Abingdon, Oxon OX14 4RN

Simultaneously published in the USA and Canada
by Routledge
711 Third Avenue, New York, NY 10017

Routledge is an imprint of the Taylor & Francis Group, an informa business

British Library Cataloguing in Publication Data
A catalogue record for this book is available from the British Library

Library of Congress Cataloging in Publication Data
A catalog record has been requested for this book

ISBN: 978-0-415-67946-6 (pbk)
ISBN: 978-0-203-80654-8 (ebk)

Typeset in Sabon by
RefineCatch Ltd, Bungay, Suffolk

Contents

List of figures

List of contributors

Soule Adam, Former MP, Benin. He is currently the Senior Budget Expert at the Parliamentary Centre (Accr).

Mark Baskin, Senior Associate, Center for International Development, Rockefeller College, University of Albany/State University of New York, United States.

Hon. John M. Cheyo, MP, Tanzania. Chair of Tanzania's Public Accounts Committee and Secretary General of SADCOPAC.

Shantayanan Devarajan, Chief Economist (Africa), World Bank, United States.

Rasheed Draman is Director of Africa Programmes at the Parliamentary Centre, Ghana.

Hon. David Ebong, MP, Uganda Chairperson, Parliamentary Forum on Climate Change.

Ben Ekeyi, Senior Legislative Aide, National Assembly of Nigeria.

Andrew Imlach, Director, Commonwealth Parliamentary Association, United Kingdom.

Sen. Joseph Karemera, Senator, Rwanda.

Hon. Beatrice Kiraso Birungi, Former MP, Uganda was the member of parliament who proposed the private member's bill establishing Uganda's Parliamentary Budget Office – the first such office outside of congressional legislative systems. She is now Deputy Executive Secretary of the East African Community.

Wanyaka Samuel Huxley is the Director of the Budget Office in Uganda.

Hon. Given Lubinda is MP in Zambia for the Kabwata Constituency (Lusaka). He is also the chairman for information and publicity for the Patriotic Front, the main opposition party in Zambia.

Chairman of the African Parliamentarians Network Against Corruption.

Hon. Anne Makinda, Speaker, Tanzanian Parliament, Constituency MP for Njombe Kusini.

Hon. Peter Oloo Aringo, Former elected MP for Alego Usoga Constituency in Nyanza Province, Kenya and also former nominated MP.

Hon. Mesfin Mengistu, MP, Ethiopia.

AbdulKarim Mohammed, Coordinator – Oil and Gas Program, Parliamentary Centre, Ghana.

Tijan Sallah, Manager, World Bank, United States.

Hon. Samuel Sallas-Mensah, Former MP, Ghana, Former Chairman of the Public Accounts Committee, currently serving as the Chief Executive Officer of Public Procurement Authority of Ghana.

Hon. William F. Shija, Secretary General of the Commonwealth Parliamentary Association, United Kingdom.

Sen. Franklin Siakor, Senator, Liberia contested the 2005 general election in Liberia as an independent candidate for the Bongo County senatorial seat. He is one of the three senators currently serving in the Liberian Senate as an independent.

Hon. Willibrod Slaa, MP, Tanzania, MP for Karatu constituency since 1995, and chairman of the Local Authorities Accounts Committee, Mr Slaa has been secretary general of the opposition party Tovuti ya Chama Cha Demokrasia na Maendeleo (CHADEMA) since 2002.

Rick Stapenhurst, Parliamentary Advisor, World Bank Institute, United States and Lecturer at McGill University, Canada.

Foreword

William F. Shija

On 6 March 1957, what British Prime Minister Harold Macmillan described three years later in Cape Town as 'the winds of change' swept into sub-Saharan Africa, Ghanaians took control of their democratic institutions as a fully independent people for the first time in the modern post-colonial era. My own country, Tanzania, and several other sub-Saharan African nations, Commonwealth and non-Commonwealth alike, followed within a few years of Ghana, to gain independence.

We took over institutions of governance which had their roots in other cultures. We experimented with different concepts of representative democracy to find a parliamentary form which would suit us. Some of us, including Ghanaians, periodically abandoned the experiment in favour of non-democratic forms, such as military rule.

In 1993, one of my predecessors as Secretary-General of the Commonwealth Parliamentary Association (CPA) took a team of experienced Commonwealth Members of Parliament (MPs) to Accra for a parliamentary seminar for the newly elected MPs of Ghana. He reported that one of their biggest challenges was a lack of experience in governance – only two of the 200 MPs had any parliamentary experience and that experience had been interrupted by 11 years of military rule.

I was appointed as Secretary-General at a Commonwealth Parliamentary Conference in 2006 in Abuja, Nigeria, as the nation was surpassing its old record of seven consecutive years of democratic governance uninterrupted by military rule.

This background shows that a few years, or even a few decades, of democratic governance is not long enough to develop effective parliamentary and governmental institutions and the public ethos to sustain them. But African parliamentarians and parliamentary staff are now in the forefront of parliamentary reform initiatives to improve the effectiveness of their institutions, to enhance their performance as professionals in the service of their people and to ensure their nations achieve the Millennium Development Goals. As Walter Rodney documented in 1973, sub-Saharan Africans have seen their countries mercilessly exploited by Europeans for centuries, consequently having to struggle to "develop" over the last half century. They are naturally intent on achieving much better results, and at greater speed, over the coming half century. They realize that national assemblies across the continent must be strengthened to do this. As this book shows, the 'winds of change' are therefore blowing across Africa again.

In addressing the 2010 Commonwealth Parliamentary Conference in Nairobi, Kenya's prime minister, Hon. Raila Odinga, MP, spurred his fellow Africans and all parliamentarians to improve the accountability of governments to save their democracies from falling back into military governments or personal dictatorships. Parliamentarians must be proactive in protecting the national institutions of democracy and applying democratic principles to prevent abuses of power. MPs find better ways to do this by sharing experiences and exchanging ideas among themselves through the CPA and other inter-parliamentary fora and in partnerships with democracy-strengthening development-oriented bodies such as the World Bank Institute (WBI) and the Parliamentary Centre. African MPs add their experiences to this pool of knowledge on parliamentary democracy through the publication of this book. By chronicling the reforms being made across Africa, the authors of these chapters reveal that African parliaments are now rapidly building on their relatively short parliamentary legacies with original ideas and adaptations that are transforming them into effective voices of the people.

Africa is currently a hotbed of parliamentary democracy. When Rwanda's Parliament joined the CPA at our Nairobi meeting, this new Commonwealth member joined 56 other national, state and provincial assemblies in Commonwealth Africa alone. One of the reasons that Rwanda decided to join the Commonwealth in 2009, despite having no historic connection with the organization, was to draw on the experience and expertise of Commonwealth parliamentarians and parliamentary officials to help its members bring all the benefits of democratic governance to its people. The special links among Commonwealth African parliaments will enable Rwanda to tap into their growing expertise in constitutional and parliamentary reform in nations with similar economic and social conditions.

The Speaker of Rwanda's lower house, the Chamber of Deputies, said recently that her Parliament looked to the network of

Commonwealth parliaments to help implement good parliamentary practices and deepen the country's democratic commitment as it rebuilds through reconciliation in the aftermath of the genocide of 1994. Joining the Commonwealth parliamentary community connects them to the experience and information they need to fulfil their commitment to good governance, justice, human rights and democracy. It also provides to the rest of Commonwealth Africa new perspectives born out of a different tradition and the horrors of an unimaginable tragedy. Sharing experiences strengthens the understanding and the resolve of all who participate, whether by reading this book or attending a seminar or conference.

In addition, this book provides a counterbalance to the popular view of Africa and its governments as the world's poorest continent; a continent where governments fail, aid disappears, people suffer and nothing improves. Africa, similar to other parts of the world, is by no means free of problems. But this book shows that its parliaments are moving decisively and effectively to resolve them and, far from failing, are in fact prominent in the global parliamentary reform movement.

The reforms described in this volume are only part of the picture of the evolution of African parliamentary governance. Last year, approximately 100 Commonwealth African parliamentarians met in the South African province of Mpumalanga to analyse their performance in the democratization of Africa, including the question of the transition between governments of different political persuasions, an issue which has in the past led to the breakdown of some democracies.

The CPA, the WBI and the Parliamentary Centre have organized workshops for representatives of West African parliamentary public accounts committees and auditors general. Participants have sought to enhance the effectiveness of their oversight of government spending. The South African provincial legislature in Limpopo sent members and officials of their public accounts committee to a special course at an Australian university to learn how to fulfil their important duties better. There are other Africans who have benefited from the course in recent years.

Members of national parliaments in the South African Development Community Parliamentary Forum seized on the CPA's 2006 initiative with the WBI, the United Nations Development Program and others to draft Benchmarks for Democratic Legislatures. The Parliamentary Forum used the CPA benchmarks as a basis to draft their own standards which their 14 parliaments should meet.

Another joint CPA–WBI initiative brought members from three African Parliaments, namely Uganda, Kenya and Rwanda, together with members from other regions late in 2010 to formulate effective ways to expand the role of parliament in preventing and resolving serious conflicts that destabilize entire nations. In the same vein, the Parliament of Kenya has set up a professionally run parliamentary study centre and is helping the parliament of Ghana to do the same.

Post-election seminars, similar to that notable 1993 seminar in the then newly demilitarized Ghana, are regularly sought by African parliaments keen that their members, newly elected as well as experienced, learn about new developments in parliamentary governance in other regions.

Also, working with the Commonwealth's intergovernmental arm, the Commonwealth Secretariat, we have held special seminars on the role of the opposition in parliament. 'Opposition' was not part of the cultural and social traditions of most African countries so for many years some countries embraced the one-party system. The transition to multi-party politics was therefore a challenge both for those who had to play the opposition role and for those who had to face opponents across the floor of their Houses. Members on both sides proved eager to learn what was expected of them, and are now actively developing ways, such as through the public exposure of ineffective programme delivery by public accounts committees, to strengthen their roles. Also, Commonwealth African parliaments have formed their own climate-change task force and their own organization for women parliamentarians under the Commonwealth Parliamentary Association.

Besides MPs, parliamentary officials across Africa are also actively involved in professional development work through attachments to other African and non-African parliaments and through workshops at the Commonwealth and African levels. At these attachments and workshops, they can help each other to understand and resolve important issues in the procedures and administration of parliament.

These programmes reinforce the underlying message in this book that African parliaments are not content to be mere rubber stamps. The continent faces enormous developmental challenges and its MPs who recognize this truth better than anyone else. The reforms demonstrate that parliamentarians are committed to ensuring that their governments solve these issues and problems quickly and permanently. They also realize that effective parliaments are necessary for this to happen. To echo this developmental drive, an African head of state recently told a CPA delegation to his country that the goal of the Commonwealth should be to help all of its member states to become 'First

World' nations. This means that, although African nations still have some considerable way to go economically and socially, their Parliaments are well on their way to becoming 'First World' governance institutions.

1   Introduction

Rick Stapenhurst and Rasheed Draman

The challenges facing African parliaments and parliamentarians, as elsewhere, are considerable. Under single-party regimes, parliaments were, in effect, extensions of the executive and their role, in many cases, was reduced to rubber-stamping policy developed by the government and the ruling party. Even when not taken to such extremes, African parliaments enjoyed little independence and exercised limited authority. Even in Africa's emerging democracies, parliaments faced legacies of patronage politics and the personalization of power – both lingering features of single-party systems which undermine the institutionalization of democratic processes. Where power is personalized, the adherence to informal rules and the reliance on contacts and connections are the norm. The already difficult task of parliamentarians, whether from the ruling or opposition parties, was complicated by the expectations of constituents, who seek personal benefits in the form of jobs, money or scholarships, in return for support.

The effective functioning of parliaments in democratic systems in Africa and elsewhere is dependent not only on the quality of the majority party and its members but also on the existence of a serious, well-informed and involved opposition. However, the role of the parliamentary opposition is not yet fully understood in many African countries, largely as a result of their recent political history. At the same time, opposition parties – as do governing parties – need to develop democratic institutional structures and advance clear political platforms and policy positions.

Relations between the executive and parliament affect how parliament functions. The balance of power between the executive and the parliament is also an issue, given that many African countries have adopted presidential systems. In some instances, the constitutional powers given to presidents are significantly greater than those afforded to parliaments. In such situations, without a clear commitment to political tolerance and space for opposing views, governments can continue to function like one-party states.

Given the limited resources and overwhelming needs, parliaments and parliamentarians in Africa have had to define their priorities and determine what their primary role will be. They have had to ascertain what they can reasonably achieve. Failure to accomplish a too-ambitious agenda runs the risk of losing credibility and public support. On the other hand, apparent inattention to pressing needs can also lead to public dissatisfaction.

Against this background, many African parliaments have an overwhelming legislative workload. They are not only faced with a backlog of laws which require revision, but also with the need for new legislation to keep up with changing demands. Trade and investment issues, climate change, scrutiny and approval of budgets and taxes, and economic policy are key areas and yet these are areas where parliamentary capacity is the most limited. The other areas of concern are accountability performance, both over the executive and its own internal accountability mechanisms as well as constituency representation.

Faced with such a difficult recent history and legacy, on the one hand, and current challenges on the other, it is surprising that parliamentary reform in Africa is perhaps more rigorous than in any other continent. African parliaments are revising constitutions and their rules of procedure to give them more power to carry out their core functions, of legislation, oversight, representation and constituency service. They are increasing their resources – establishing independent parliamentary service commissions with the power to hire, promote and fire staff, building offices for MPs and staff in parliament itself and in the constituencies, and building parliamentary libraries and research services – all aimed at making their institution a relevant and viable institution for the twenty-first century. While these reforms are not yet widespread across the continent, parliaments in some countries are asserting their independence as policymakers, as overseers of government and as the guardian of citizens' rights and needs.

Yet, until very recently, this wave of African parliamentary reform went largely unnoticed outside of Africa. Groundbreaking was Joel Barkan's book *Legislative Power in Emerging African Democracies*, in which it was argued that some African countries are leading the way in legislative reform. Barkan concluded that a combination of two or more of six variables explain the emergence, or otherwise, of reform in a particular legislature and how successful such reform might be. The six variables are:

- The presence of committed 'reformers' within parliament who understand the changes required and who are willing to lead their fellow MPs to make those changes;
- A large and talent-laden civil society that sees the imperative of improving parliamentary performance as a key component of democratic development;
- Lingering neo-patrimonialism, which seeks to limit parliamentary development and retain power in the hands of the executive;
- The attitudes of the chief presiding officer (Speaker or President) and chief administrative officer (Clerk or Secretary General) of parliament, and whether they support or oppose reforms;
- Whether political parties are strong or weak, although here Barkan is equivocal about whether strong parties promote or limit reform;
- Electoral system, where a proportional representation system, especially with party lists, can limit the freedom of MPs to act independently.

That African parliaments are reforming into institutions to be reckoned with should not be completely surprising. In 2009, Steven Fish and Martin Kroenig published *The Handbook of National Legislatures*. In their ranking of nearly 160 national parliaments, some African parliaments, at least, scored well: Mauritius, South Africa Benin, Lesotho, Ethiopia, Namibia and Niger were in the top two quartiles, while Ghana, Nigeria, Rwanda, Angola and Botswana were 'bubbling under'.

This book presents some of the recent reforms in selected African parliaments – Benin, Ethiopia, Ghana, Kenya, Liberia, Nigeria, Rwanda, Tanzania, Uganda and Zambia. It also presents some cross-cutting innovations by African parliaments – in fighting corruption, in providing development to constituents, in overseeing petroleum resources and in combating climate change. It is unique, in that for the most part the chapters are written by reform-minded African MPs themselves – to simplify, the book is 'by MPs for MPs' as well as for those in international institutions that support parliamentary development and scholars interested in legislative development.

The book is divided into two parts: country case studies and cross-cutting themes. In the former, MPs tell of the reforms in their parliaments regarding changes to standing orders, outreach to constituents and civil society better oversight of government, gender equality and the roles that their institutions have played in post-conflict reconstruction. In the latter, MPs tell of the continent-wide initiatives that have brought African parliaments to the fore of reducing corruption, overseeing petroleum resources, combating climate change and providing constituency service.

Our goal in this book is twofold. First, we want to provide a platform from which Africa's leading reform-minded MPs can address their peers across Africa and around the world. And second, we want to highlight to legislative studies scholars and practitioners alike the very real progress made by some African parliaments in reforming themselves into viable and vital institutions.

2 Engaging civil society
Ghana's first public PAC hearing

Samuel Sallas-Mensah

Introduction to the Ghanaian Parliament

The 1992 Constitution provided for a president and a single-chamber parliament based on a multi-party system, both elected every four years. Under the Constitution, the president appoints ministers of state to the executive, with the requirement that more than half come from the list of MPs. This results in a hybrid political system, with elements of both presidential and parliamentary governance.

The Parliament, which comprises elected MPs, is headed by the Speaker, who is the leader of the House and an important link between the legislature and the executive. The Speaker is assisted by a parliamentary service that provides services to Parliament and is headed by the Clerk of Parliament. The mandate of the parliamentary service is to facilitate the work of Parliament, and it has almost 500 permanent employees.

Parliament performs its legislative role by considering and approving, amending or rejecting legislative proposals brought by the executive. Legislative proposals are considered first by the Parliament as a whole, before being considered in greater detail by the relevant committee. Finally, Parliament approves or rejects the proposal in plenary. Once Parliament has approved a proposal, presidential assent is required before the bill becomes law.

Parliament performs its oversight role primarily through the work of committees. Standing committees are constituted at the first meeting of Parliament and are meant to facilitate the on-going concern of the House. Select committees have the task of overseeing the policies and practices of ministers, departments and agencies (MDAs) of government.

The Public Accounts Committee

The Public Accounts Committee (PAC) is a standing committee of Parliament. Comprising 25 MPs, and chaired by a member of the opposition, it is responsible for reviewing the auditor-general's (AGs) reports. The PAC's chairman is necessarily from the minority group in Parliament, which enhances PAC's performance because there is an added incentive to check the working powers of the executive. According to the Standing Orders of Parliament (2000) its task is 'the examination of the audited accounts showing the appropriation of the sums granted by Parliament to meet the public expenditure of the Government and of such other accounts laid before parliament.' The AG's reports are submitted to Parliament, where they are reviewed by the PAC. The PAC examines the audited accounts and the AG's report. The PAC's sessions are private, but PAC reports to the Speaker are on public record. On the basis of the examination it makes recommendations to the House. The recommendations are then discussed in Parliament and if accepted, they are forwarded to the executive to be implemented.

The PAC is empowered to question the rationale behind the use of public funds, and if policies that are used to justify the usage of funds do not seem to be interpreted appropriately, the PAC can undertake a hearing and call witnesses to testify on the accounts.

The way to a public hearing

The PAC has the power to summon anybody, even persons residing outside of the country. If called to appear as a witness, one is required by law to testify, and neglect will result in arrest and prosecution. When it comes to summoning witnesses, the PAC has the same powers as the High Court. As per Standing Order 199 of Parliament, committee meetings are in camera, unless the chairman of the committee decides otherwise; from 2003 up to 2006 PAC hearings were held in camera. Every chairman has his own style, and when I became Chairman of the PAC in 2005, I strongly felt that it was time to increase transparency and give the public the opportunity of knowing and assessing how their tax money was being spent.

Of concern to me was that there was insufficient response to the call to testify, or to following up on the recommendations from the PAC. For instance, while conducting a check on the PAC's work up until 2005, I found that PAC recommendations had never been implemented in practice.

I reasoned that the same style of hearings (i.e. in camera) would lead to the same unsatisfactory outcomes. After attending capacity-building efforts of external donors, I came to the conclusion that the next PAC hearing should not be in camera, but in public. The road to actually organizing this public hearing was long, and it took a lot of time, effort and convincing to overcome certain obstacles.

The most difficult part of organizing the public hearing was to sell the idea to other members. For instance, it was hard to convince Committee members as most of them belong to the government party. I spent a lot of time informing my fellow PAC members and other politicians about the advantages of a public hearing, and how it would increase accountability and transparency. I often talked to certain members in private. I tried to convince them of the advantages of transparency and checks on financial management. Many of the ministers did not know what was going on even in their own department, so transparency and oversight were in their interests as well. If members were still not willing to support my idea of a public PAC hearing, my final argument was that I would inform the public and the media of their unwillingness to participate. I was determined to reach my goal, and did not want to be held back by anyone.

It also took some time to have the Speaker of the House agreeing to the public hearing. This was mainly related to budgetary issues; neither Parliament nor the PAC had sufficient funds to undertake such a demanding event. To solve this issue, I turned to the Parliamentary Centre and other donors, who then agreed on providing funds to organize and execute the hearing.

With the most important MPs convinced and some funds to work with, it was now time to organize some study tours to countries where PAC hearings are already public. With a total of five PAC members, carefully divided between government and opposition parties, and with help of the World Bank Institute, we travelled to South Africa and Australia to learn about how public hearings are conducted in those countries.

We then used the donor funds to train the Ghanaian media and prepare them for the hearing. It was necessary that the media was up to date on public management processes and financial procedures, so that they knew what the hearing was about, and what to report on.

We also organized trainings for our own staff, to clarify relevant aspects of public financial management and parliamentary processes. The Ghanaian PAC lacks both logistical and human-resource capacity, and a dedicated PAC staff is difficult to find. Like most other committees, the PAC has four permanent staff officials. This includes one researcher, so overall research capacity is low. MPs are often not fully prepared for meetings and clerks are not up to date. A knowledgeable chairman will use his management and personal skills to create respect within the committee first. I then used this respect to discipline the Committee members by demanding that they come to the meetings prepared and on time. For example, not showing up for a meeting was unacceptable for me.

Lastly, we set up training and meetings for the AG's staff. The AG would be called as a witness during the hearing. The AG did not have to provide any opening remarks or an executive summary of the AG report; his only task was to answer questions from the Public Accounts Committee and to explain important matters in further detail. The pre-briefings and opportunities for questions we had with the AG and his staff were necessary for both parties to understand and be fully aware of the issues. It also allowed us to concentrate only on the most critical matters during the hearing. The PAC works closely with the AG on a regular basis and depends on the AG for its work. It is therefore imperative that the trust between the two parties is maintained, even when addressing sensitive issues. Because the integrity of the AG is at stake when possible cases of corruption are discussed in public, private pre-briefings proved to be a useful tool for the AG to know what could be expected at the hearing.

This careful planning and preparation of different stakeholders was necessary to make the hearing a success. It was also the reason the AG 2004 report was discussed only in 2007. Everybody involved had to be aware of the benefits of this hearing, which questions to ask, and which pitfalls to avoid. Without the right capacity in place I was afraid the hearing might not be taken seriously, which would have significantly hampered Parliament's and the PAC's credibility.

PAC hearings going public

In October 2007 the PAC held its first public hearing and discussed the Reports of the AG on the Public Accounts of Ghana for the year ended 31st December 2004 for Ministries, Departments and Agencies of the Central Governance. Prior to the public hearing held by the Public Accounts Committee in 2007, the only committee meetings that had been held in public were those of the Appointments Committee of Parliament. The public hearing by the Committee was aimed at increasing transparency, strengthening the accountability process in the public service, and boosting the confidence and support of the public in Parliament. It was also an opportunity for the public to feed the PAC with information on how some projects or expenditures of government were managed. Through advertisements in newspapers, television and discussion platforms the general public and civil society were invited to the hearing. Through both electronic and written media we had asked for input from anyone that had information on the matters on the agenda, with the possibility for people to testify in public if they wanted to. Both CSOs and the general public responded to our advertisements, but attended the hearing as observers, not as witnesses. The hearing attracted quite a crowd, and the general public and civil society organizations like the Parliamentary Centre and the Ghana Integrity Initiative were present.

During the public hearing

The hearing addressed many issues. The main ones are listed below:

1   The Attorney-General had to explain why two public servants who had been charged with embezzlement of government funds in 2002 by falsifying some records and forging signatures still had not been prosecuted. The case was still pending at the Attorney General's office for further advice. The PAC also called the Inspector General of Police to explain similar cases;
2   The PAC called the Chief of Justice to set up the Financial Administrative Tribunal to deal with such prosecutions;
3   The Minister of Tourism and his Chief Director appeared before the PAC to explain improper accountability of resources allocated to the ministry. Vouchers did not accompany monies paid, and contracts awarded were not documented. The PAC was told that the ministry did not have its own internal audit system. The ministry was ordered to refund the 15 per cent of Cedi 14.5 million paid to an agency for an additional work on an advertising project, and the PAC ordered further investigations into a two-billion-Cedi mosquito-spraying exercise;
4   The Ministry of Trade and Industry, Private Sector Development and President's Special Initiative was call to answer questions on several findings from the AG's report. Among many others, some of the abuses of public funds turned out to be:

  •   The PAC heard how 2153 garments, worth Cedi 995 million, were distributed free of charge to unknown people by the Ministry of Trade, Industry, Private Sector Development and Presidential Special Initiative. The distribution list could not be produced for verification by the audit team;

- The PAC found out about a double payment of Cedi 185.7 million made by the ministry to a private company for the same service;
- The PAC pointed to the double monthly salary of a government official, whom the PAC recommended be terminated and efforts be made to recover the salary payments made;
- A company was awarded 14 contracts of Cedi 1.4 billion through single sourcing instead of competitive bidding (as required by the Public Procurement Act, 2003);
- The ministry paid Cedi 1.36 billion to personnel as fees and salaries from Government of Ghana funds. During investigations, the AG could not ascertain the basis for the payments. The PAC ordered the ministry to provide the list of persons who benefited from the salaries and fees;
- The PAC had asked the AG to resolve issues addressed in earlier PAC reports but that had not been taken on sufficiently.

The chair of the Committee determines who will be invited to the hearing. I invited both the public and private media. In the invitation process and the preparation stage (the media was briefed on all issues before the hearing) the public and private media partners were given the same treatment. Both broadcasted the hearing on national TV, however during the hearing the Ghana Broadcasting Corporation (GBC – the nation's public broadcaster), had resumed live broadcasting. The GBC started live coverage, but stopped after just a couple of hours. The GBC cites budgetary constraints as the reason, however I believe the real reason for shutdown was that ministers were called to testify. Luckily the private media continued to report on the hearing until the end.

The hearing evidenced that public procurement procedures were not followed according to the law. Therefore the PAC recommended applying competitive bidding to call contracts, in order to enhance transparency, efficiency and fair prices in the awarding of contracts. The report also recommended that the auditors be careful and thorough in their work, and properly maintain their papers. The hearing had proven that data management and evaluations of MDAs and the AG were insufficient. Well-organized and independent audit systems contribute to a better and more transparent control of the activities of the public-sector institutions, which also enhances economic efficiency and effectiveness. With effective monitoring and tracking of public expenditures on the AG's side, some issues addressed in the PAC hearing could have been sorted out by the AG's office itself.

On cases of misuse of public funds, the accounts officers were summoned to retrieve the money within two months, or be surcharged.

Implementation, follow-up, and results

The recommendations were sent to Parliament and were debated extensively. Parliament reached consensus on the report and almost all recommendations were accepted. Parliament's voting was in favor of the report, so MDAs were required to follow up the recommendations made. Since then, records of the actions undertaken on the recommendations have being kept. The records show that the audited entities are taking action on PAC reports. Six months after the hearing the PAC decided to take a look at the implementation of its recommendations, and found very positive results. A total of USD 40 million was brought back to the national budget after the first public hearing. Government officials were taken to trial for misuse of public funds, and some of the prosecution procedures are still ongoing. However, one recommendation, the establishment of the Financial Administration Tribunal (which was a requirement of the Financial Administration Act of 2003 as well) for handling these trials has not made much progress yet because of financial constraints and lack of political will.

At the time of writing, the PAC does not yet have any interim hearings scheduled to discuss follow-up. However, the new government of 2008 introduced ongoing work to the new PAC. Implementation and follow-up of recommendations were a key priority, and the PAC recommends to the AG that he prioritize its recommendations. The AG is expected to look into the recommendations before taking on any other projects. For a check on implementation of the recommendations the PAC asks the AG for information directly. There is a steering committee/liaison office to handle the contact and ongoing projects between the PAC and the AG. The two parties share information on a regular basis. However, there is no structural or formal relationship or formal requirements. Whenever needed, a phone call or visit to each other's office is always possible.

One of the implications the series of public hearings has had is that MDA representatives are afraid to be asked to appear before the PAC for questioning in public in the future. They know their documents and work processes are being checked extensively, which is a huge incentive for honest governance and good record-keeping. More importantly, one of the indirect results of the hearing was that the public came to realize the extent of the powers of the Parliament.

The public hearing was not an occasional event: in 2008 our PAC organized the second public hearing and covered the 2006 AG report. The next open hearing, under the leadership of the extremely competent new PAC Chairman, took place in July 2009. It is imperative that my successor keeps up the momentum for the public hearing. The fear is that because of the election year, the AG's office has not been keeping its data up to date, and many of its reports didn't make it to Parliament. The PAC should insist that the AG clears this backload and does not get stuck behind.

Crucial factors of success

After the hearing, at the end of the year, we organized a peer-review meeting to discuss and debrief about the hearing and formulate lessons learned for future practices. The meeting was funded by the World Bank Institute and the Parliamentary Centre, and involved all stakeholders again.

The lessons learned were positive: the training of stakeholders and collaboration with important governance institutions were perceived as critical and our efforts were praised. Media attention for the hearing proved crucial as well. However, I would advise my successor to try to avoid too much media attention in the day-to-day working of the PAC and in the run-up to the annual hearing. The PAC is supposed to serve the Parliament and its constituents, independent of personal party preference. But the Chair of the PAC belongs to the opposition party, and it is often the chair who is asked to respond to the media. Therefore it might seem sometimes as if the Chair is speaking on behalf of his party, politicizing certain issues. One can avoid accusations of party bias by letting other members of the PAC respond to media requests. It might also be a good idea to let the Chair and his Deputy conduct an interview together. Also, the timing of media interviews should not interfere with any other current political issues and engagements. The risk of politicizing the PAC's topics is then too high.

The effectiveness of Parliament depends partly upon the resources available, such as salaries of MPs and parliamentary staff, all types of infrastructure, and access to information. Lack of equipment like computers, offices and vehicles may weaken parliamentary committees. The capacity may be further hampered by the absence of trained staff. A lack of resources (including sufficient office accommodation) prevents the PAC from being more comprehensive or from holding more regular sessions. Ghana's Parliament and the PAC operate in a challenging context. They are dependent on the executive for their institutional resources. Although there has been a substantial increase in the volume of resources provided to Parliament by the government in recent years, in practice the Ghanaian Parliament often receives fewer resources than it requests, and resources are sometimes delayed. The budget of the PAC is currently only USD 60,000 per year. The workload of the PAC has increased considerably in terms of number of accounts audited, but this has not been sufficiently reflected in the PAC's budget. In fact, in real terms resources have been reduced. In the case of the Ghanaian PAC, many of these problems are addressed by donor funding from the European Commission, African Development Bank, the Department for International Development (DfID), the Parliamentary Centre, and the World Bank Institute. Projects involve training in the budget process and financial audits, performance audit and planning, budgeting and management information systems. Computers and vehicles to enhance operations have also been provided. In the future Parliament might be increasing its funding for the PAC as there are signs the PAC will be a priority focus.

In the developed world where governments are transparent, civil society led the crusade in reaching such a high point. Unfortunately, in Africa and most developing countries, civil society appears rather docile. Even though there has been a steady growth in civil-society activism in Ghana since the return to democratic governance, there is still a need to accelerate the activism if we are to achieve the level of transparency we all desire.

I must admit that there is still a lot to be done, especially in the area of implementing and enforcing existing financial laws. Parliament should amend its standing orders to allow the PAC to institute independent investigations into information that has been brought to the PACs attention by whistle-blowers. Currently, the PAC can investigate matters outside the AG's report, but only if the matter has been referred to the Committee by the Speaker of Parliament. Because of the nationwide attention to the public hearings, the PAC has been receiving many complaints from whistle-blowers, but it is unable to act on them.

It is also important that a Freedom of Information (FOI) Bill is enacted to complement the Whistle Blowers Act in our effort to achieve a transparent and corruption-free administration. Effective collaboration with the media is also imperative in this process. The recent public hearing of the PAC generated lots of interest in the activities of government by the public and the Committee has already started receiving some whistle-blowers on activities of public servants, but I am sure the number of cases would be much higher had the FOI

Act been enacted. Currently, the FOI has been drafted and the goal is that it will be brought to Parliament to debate and vote on in the near future.

Finally I would argue that the law should be amended to make the auditor-general more independent from the executive. Currently the AG is directly appointed by the president, but because the AG has to report to Parliament, I don't see why he shouldn't be appointed by Parliament as well.

3 Parliamentary research and information – the Ugandan Parliament's Budget Office and Parliamentary Budget Committee

Beatrice Kiraso Birungi
with Wanyaka Samuel Huxley

An Act of Parliament established Uganda's Parliamentary Budget Office (PBO) on 27 February 2001, although the provisions of the act only came into force on 1 July 2001 when the president assented to the bill. The objective of the act was to 'Provide for and regulate the budgetary processes for a systematic and efficient budgetary processes and other matters connected therewith.' The bill was initiated as a private member's bill by the Chairpersons of the Committee on Finance, Planning & Economic Development and the Committee of National Economy and scrutinized by the relevant committee of Parliament (the Committee of Finance, Planning & Economic Development). This Committee examined the bill and made a lot of improvements, clearly prescribing responsibilities and timelines for the various stakeholders in the budget-making and execution process.

The aim of the bill was to address the fact that traditionally Parliament only played a passive role in the budgetary process – approving rather than proactively shaping/scrutinizing the budget (Articles 155 and 156 of the 1995 Constitution). Support for the establishment of the Parliamentary Budget Office arose out of parliamentary capacity-building meetings, seminars and conferences, at which members of parliament realized that Parliament, as a whole, needed to play a more active role in the budget-making process. Specifically, it became apparent that in the past Parliament had been a mere 'rubber stamp' and that information provided to Parliament on budget-related matters was generally inadequate. Parliamentarians were ordinarily kept ignorant on issues such as local resource revenue, foreign inflows for budget support or project financing, national expenditure priority areas and macroeconomic statistics.

It was agreed in principle that as the peoples' representatives, members of parliament (MPs) should become more effective and accountable in their oversight role of the budget – one most important tool by which they could influence the economic and social development policies of the country.

The executive, on the other hand, was clearly not keen on allowing Parliament more participation, and therefore restricted the information received by Parliament. It is for this reason that the Budget Bill faced a lot of resistance. Whereas other bills, after being introduced into Parliament, took on average three weeks between the first and second reading, the Budget Bill took about eight months from the time it was first introduced to the time it was, finally, passed. The Uganda Constitution (Article 93) dictates that Parliament shall not introduce a motion (including an amendment) that would impose a charge on the Consolidated Fund. The Budget Bill if passed would establish the Budget Office and a Budget Committee and these two would require extra funding, therefore imposing a charge on the consolidated fund.

The Government conveniently used this Constitutional provision as a good excuse to reject the bill. After some months of negotiation between the government, led by the Ministry of Finance, and Parliament, led by the two Committee Chairpersons, the Government agreed to reintroduce the bill as a government bill. This never happened, as clearly Government was not in favor of Parliament scrutinizing the Budget. Demands by Parliament to undertake more Budget scrutiny were described as interference in the work of the executive and an abuse to separation of powers provided for in the Constitution.

About two months of lobbying other members of parliament and sensitizing them of the need for Parliament to scrutinize the Budget more effectively produced a growing consensus among members of parliament that the establishment of a Parliamentary Budget Office would be a good idea. It was agreed that, Article 93 of the Constitution notwithstanding, the private member's bill should be reintroduced, regardless of whether Government was agreeable or not, and that Parliament would pass it. After all, the Constitution clearly states that if for one reason or another the President refused to assent to a bill, but Parliament by majority so decides, it will become law.

The bill was reintroduced by the Hon. Isaac Musumba, Chairperson of the Committee on National Economy and committed to the Committee of Finance, Planning & Economic Development chaired by Hon. Beatrice Kiraso. The two committees worked together to come up with the final bill which was allowed by the Speaker to be read the second time and in February 2001 passed by overwhelming majority.

The structure of the Parliament of Uganda

Until September 2005, when the Uganda Constitution was amended to open up for political pluralism, Uganda was governed under a 'Movement system', where leaders were elected on the basis of individual merit. Therefore, there was no cohesive government or opposition support in Parliament. Thus, it was easier for members of parliament to support a bill which strengthened Parliament as an institution. As with most parliaments around the world the Uganda Parliament elected from among its members a Speaker and Deputy Speaker, they too would be non-partisan. It is presumed therefore that the Speaker and Deputy Speaker would also be elected on merit considering qualifications and competence and the ability to serve the interests of Parliament. Although there were a few members of parliament who considered themselves as the de facto opposition – basically because they preferred a multi-party system to the movement system – the majority of Parliament acted in a non-partisan, independent manner.

For efficient discharge of its functions, Parliament operates through committees, which make reports for consideration and adoption by the whole House. The committees do most of the detailed work on bills and other submissions. The Rules of Procedure of the Parliament of Uganda provide for standing committees, sessional committees and ad hoc or select committees. Standing committees' membership lasts for a period of half the term of Parliament, that is, two and a half years, while sessional committees are constituted in every session, which is one year.

The Speaker, on the other hand, constitutes ad hoc or select committees for a specific purpose and for a prescribed period of time, usually a few months. A member of parliament cannot belong to more than one standing committee and one sessional committee, but can serve on one standing and one sessional committee at a time.

Standing committees deal with issues that are cross-cutting in nature (e.g. the public accounts, rules and privileges of Parliament, approval of presidential appointments and so on). The sessional committees oversee the various ministries/sectors of government under their jurisdiction. The relevant ministers present/defend their policies and activities before their corresponding committees. There are thirteen sessional committees, some of which combine two or more ministries and it is these sessional committees under the Budget Act which scrutinize individual ministries' budgets and report to the Budget Committee.

The Budget Act provides for a Budget Committee, which is a standing committee of Parliament, and what distinguishes it from other committees is that, unlike other committees which were created by the Parliamentary Rules of Procedure, the Budget Committee was created by an act of parliament. Another important attribute of the Budget Committee is that all chairpersons of other committees (standing and sessional) are ex-officio members of the Budget Committee. This makes it easier for the Committee to receive reports from other committees on the Budget and related matters and to give the Budget Committee a wider and total picture of the national Budget and the government programmes and activities being carried out in the various sectors. The major functions carried out by the Budget Committee are prescribed in the Act, Section 19(1) and (2).

The Parliamentary Budget Office

Section 20 and 21 of the Budget Act set up the Parliamentary Budget Office (PBO). The office consists of economists with expertise in macroeconomics, data analysis, fiscal and tax policy. The initial structure provided for 11 posts, but, due to the high demand for the services of the PBO, there are now 21 experts. The PBO is headed by a director. While most of the positions were filled, to date the office has lost over 40 per cent of the staff due to better opportunities (salaries) elsewhere. Budget constraints also continue to limit the work of the PBO. Given the anticipated growth in the demand for the PBO's services there is, therefore, an urgent need to implement strategies to improve staff retention rates. The structure of the PBO is hereby attached as Figure 3.1.

The resistance, from the government, to having in place a budget act and, therefore, a Budget Office and Budget Committee, did not stop even after the law was passed. Budget constraints affected the initial setting up and running of the PBO. After the 2001 general elections, the Seventh Parliament came into being; Ms. Kiraso Beatrice who had initiated the Budget Bill during the Sixth Parliament was elected the first chairperson of the Budget Committee. The chairperson sought assistance from USAID, which at that time had an ongoing capacity-building programme for Parliament. The special request to assist in setting up the PBO was also shared with other donor agencies. In the end USAID, DfID, GTZ, EU, The World Bank and NORAD[1] all provided assistance in the form of furniture, computers and software, as well as the initial allowances for the PBO's officers. Within one year of the PBO's inception the Parliamentary Commission

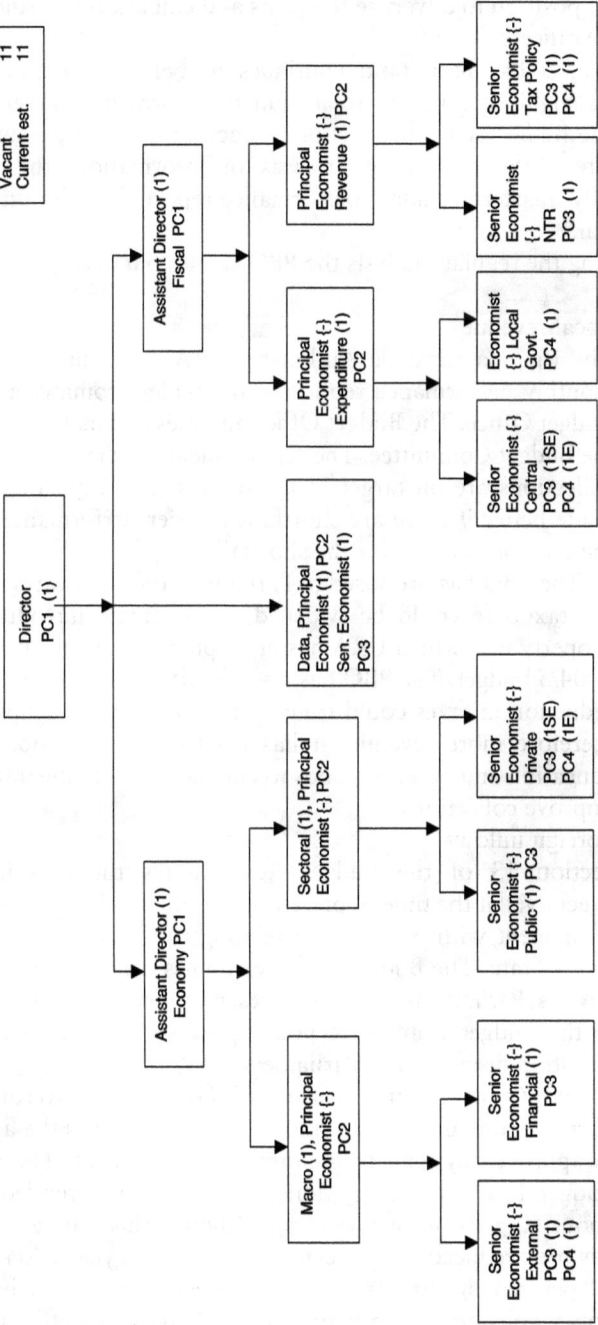

Figure 3.1 Parliamentary Budget Office (PBO)

was in a position to advertise the posts and embark on recruitment of the PBO officers.

The PBO has been (and continues to be) non-partisan, objective and highly committed to its functions provided under Section 21 of the Budget Act. The level of interaction with the parliamentary committees, the quality of analysis of information, the periodic (normally quarterly) budget performance reports have become better each year.

Among the regular analysis the PBO carries out are:

(i) Local revenue
     The Uganda Revenue Authority (URA) is required to submit monthly performance reports to the budget committee and the Budget Office. The Budget Office analyses and makes reports for the Budget Committee. The reports identify whether the revenue collections are on target, if the targets were right or could be made better if there are shortfalls or over performance and on the possible reasons for the shortfalls.

     The PBO has proposed to Parliament different ways in which the tax base could be widened, for example introduction of property tax, which URA has attempted to implement since the 2004/5 budget. The PBO has also identified possible areas where reduction in taxes could trigger off increased consumption and therefore more revenue. It has participated to proposing tax education and other methods to enhance tax administration and improve collections.

(ii) Foreign inflows
     Section 13 of the Budget Act requires the president (the executive) at the time of presenting the annual budget to provide Parliament with information relating to the total indebtedness of the State. The Budget Office examines these submissions and advises Parliament on these presentations and makes reports to the Budget Committee pointing out issues, which need the attention/discussion of Parliament.

     The Constitution (Article 159(1)) allows government to borrow from any source, but Article 159(2) gives the authority to approve any loan or guarantee to Parliament. The national Budget has, for a long time, been externally funded (up to about 50 per cent of revenues). Although this source of income has been reduced, 42 per cent in the financial year 2004/05, and 23 per cent in 2010/11. In fact the entire recurrent budget is now wholly domestically funded. PBO advises on efficient forms of external financing of the budget, including on the conditionalities, disbursement and absorption of the funds. The PBO monitors and reports on such disbursements from both multilateral and bilateral donors in order to point out possible issues that would require government to reprioritize on its expenditures.

PBO has greatly improved the relevant committee's capacity to understand the loan agreements between government and the donors, so Parliament no longer approves loans without effective scrutiny. Parliament is now in position to question or even request government to renegotiate provisions that are found not to be favourable.

(iii) Expenditure

Section 6 of the Budget Act requires each minister to submit, to Parliament, by the thirtieth day of June of each financial year an expenditure policy statement. This statement, among other things, is expected to outline the funds appropriated for the relevant ministry (for that financial year) and how much the ministry spent and what these resources were used for.

The PBO then reconciles/scrutinizes the releases of funds (or in some ministries the supplementary) with the total budget performance, and if there are discrepancies brings this to the notice of the budget committee. The PBO has also developed modules – which are still simple – that committees use to monitor the performance of the sectors they oversee. Whereas ministries are, by law, required to submit annual policy statements, the PBO has been producing quarterly budget performance reports. This process has enabled Parliament to follow the general budget performance and particular sector performance throughout the year.

(iv) Economic indicators

The PBO can, at any given time, undertake an independent investigation and generate a report regarding the performance of the economy. Parliament, since the PBO was established, is able to follow up on the implications of the executive's macroeconomic policies, receive independent information on poverty trends, and verify figures given by government regarding economic growth. Parliament is now able to debate, from an informed position, the socio-economic trends and, as is required by the Budget Act Section 11, analyze programmes and policy issues that affect the national Budget and economy and where necessary recommend alternative approaches to the government.

Furthermore, at the close of each financial year, the Parliamentary Budget Office produces a record of whether the government has implemented Parliament's recommendations. This has greatly improved the quality of the oversight role and enhanced accountability on the part of government and consequently, on the part of members of parliament to their constituents.

The budget cycle

The Uganda Budget, as per Article 155(1) of the Constitution, is prepared and presented before Parliament no later than the fifteenth day before the commencement of the financial year. The financial year commences 1 July.

Prior to the coming into effect of the Budget Act, Parliament would receive the Budget when it was presented on or about the fifteenth day of June in each financial year, committees would look at the policy statements of their relevant ministries, present reports to Parliament which would, ordinarily, pass the Budget by the end of October. Effective in 2001, when the Budget Act came into force, Parliament started participating more actively in the Budget process, by setting of expenditure priorities both for the following financial year and for the three years to follow – Medium Term Expenditure Frameworks (MTEF).

Amongst the most important changes which clearly demonstrate how parliament's authority has been enhanced by the PBO are the facts that:

(i) Whereas, prior to 2001, Parliament would receive the budget figures at the time the budget is read, now the Act requires the president (represented by the Ministry of Finance) to submit the **indicative** and **preliminary** revenue and expenditure framework of government for the next financial year by 1 April (Budget Act Section 4(2)). The indicative figures are then committed by the speaker to the Budget Committee and all sessional committees. Sessional committees consider, discuss and review the indicative allocations to the sectors under their jurisdictions and prepare reports, which are submitted, to the Budget Committee, by 25 April. During the time when sessional committees are reviewing the indicative allocations an economist from the PBO is attached to each committee to give guidance and assist by pointing out areas of importance or discrepancy with earlier approved policies.

(ii) Whereas the Constitution clearly requires that the president submit, to Parliament, fiscal and monetary programs, as well as estimates of revenue and expenditure covering periods exceeding one year, this had never happened prior to the coming into effect of the Budget Act. The Budget Act (Section 4(1)) emphasizes this Constitutional requirement. Parliament has therefore not only received annual estimates but also estimates of the three consecutive years. The budget committee, with the assistance of expert scrutiny from the PBO, then reports to Parliament pointing out any inconsistencies, policy changes and their justification (or lack of it), plus revenue and expenditure projections for the following three years.

Members of parliament are now able to inform their constituents more authoritatively on government programs with a clearer indication of when they will be implemented.

(iii) Policy statements, which used to be submitted any time before the budget is passed, are now submitted by 30 June, giving ample time for their consideration. This gives enough time for sessional committees to scrutinize them and report to Parliament. Again, there's an official from the PBO attached to each Sessional committee as they scrutinize the policy statements, which by law (Section 6(2)), are expected to reflect specific data on value for money and the extent of achievement of the objective targets on money received and spent by each sector. The standardization of the policy statement was done by the PBO together with the Ministry of Finance and approved by the Budget Committee.

(iv) It was recognized that there were pieces of legislation which, when passed during a financial year, distort the budget, such as bills and motions whose implementation would require amounts of funding not previously budgeted for. The Budget Act (Section (10)) requires that every bill introduced in Parliament shall be accompanied by a prediction of its financial implications. The certificate of financial implications is tabled together with the bill on its first reading and is committed to the relevant sessional committee along with the bill. The committees then seek the expertise of the PBO to verify the accuracy of these certificates and advise on the implications of the Budget for the relevant financial year.

(v) Section 11 of the Act mandates Parliament to analyze programmes and policy issues that affect the national Budget and economy and, where necessary, recommend alternative approaches to government. Parliament would not be able to do this without the assistance of the PBO, which prepares economic performance reports on a quarterly basis. As already mentioned, these include revenue as well as expenditure-related issues.

(vi)   While the Constitution provides for supplementary expenditure over and above what Parliament has appropriated, before the Budget Act came into force these expenditures were significant – sometimes up to 20 per cent of the initial Budget. This distortion is addressed in Section 12 of the Budget Act and the PBO assists the Budget Committee to analyze the figures and ensure that the supplementary expenditure is within the 3 per cent of the initial Budget (as prescribed by law). The PBO is also in constant touch with the various ministries in order to ensure that budget execution is approved by Parliament. Parliament is now able to receive reports regarding financial reallocations within ministries or departments, and across sectors. Such timely information is relevant for Parliament in order to keep track of whether there is budgetary discipline in different segments of the executive.

(vii)   The reports from the President, regarding the total indebtedness of the state, are scrutinized by the PBO, a more simplified and easy to understand analysis is then prepared for the Budget Committee which in turn presents a report to Parliament. The Uganda Parliamentary Budget Office in doing all the above has carried out its important functions, namely:

- Providing economic forecasts;
- Formulating baseline estimates;
- Building a database of social and economic indicators;
- Assisting Parliament to analyze the national Budget and national economy;
- Assisting Parliament to analyze the MTEF.

The PBO has also been key in identifying alternative policy approaches and presented such modules especially on taxation to the relevant committees. The non-partisan and professional nature of the unit has enabled it to perform the above functions to the satisfaction of Parliament as well as the executive. The executive now recognizes and appreciates that Parliament is able to deal with budget issues on the same footing.

Successes

With the assistance of the PBO, the budget process has been demysti-fied. What was earlier overlooked as a specialized, difficult and boring area – dealing with figures – has now become simpler, more interesting and easier to understand. Budget discussions are now livelier, both inside and outside Parliament.

The strict measures prescribed in the Act on how to deal with the Budget have assisted in making Budget formulation and execution more transparent, participatory and inclusive. Since all parliamentary committee meetings are open to the press and the public, Budget-related issues are now understood by most of the population.

The participation of members of parliament, as the peoples' representatives, has enhanced the creditability of the Budget as there is now perceived to be more ownership of the process. Other stakeholders like civil society organisations and the donor community, though not specified in the Act, are able to interact with the committees during the Budget-discussion stage. In fact interest groups like manufactures, exporters, farmers and so on that are affected by tax measures are accommodated by Parliament with better understanding of their issues.

The timelines in the Budget Act have improved the discipline in preparation as well as execution of the Budget. Though at first there was resistance from the executive, now each player appreciates their roles, those of others and the time frames. Government compliance has improved, and accountability has been promoted.

Finally, Parliament is now able to participate and contribute during public expenditure review meetings and formulation of poverty reduction programmes. All in all, the ownership between the executive and Parliament has greatly improved.

Challenges

In performing its duties outlined above, the PBO has faced a number of challenges. Key among them are the following:

(i) **Information:** the Budget Committee and PBO have proposed having IT connectivity to the key centres where Budget-related information could be accessed by the PBO more easily and quickly. However, this has not happened. Therefore, the PBO relies on information provided by other centres e.g. the Ministry of Finance, Bank of Uganda, Uganda Bureau of Statistics, and has no effective means of cross-checking the information provided. There are times when information furnished to the PBO has been found to be inaccurate, inadequate and sometimes not timely.

(ii)   **Establishment structure:** Since it was revised to provide for more officers in the PBO, some posts have remained vacant because of budget constraints and the large staff turnover. The existing officers, therefore, are faced with a very heavy workload and they work longer hours, especially during the Budget scrutiny period.

(iii) **Cooperation:** While cooperation with government departments/sectors has generally improved, some ministries either deliberately or out of incompetence do not provide the PBO with the information it requires to assist Parliament with developing its comprehensive budget reports.

(iv)   **Discrimination/bureaucracy:** Surprisingly, the PBO suffers some extent of discrimination from the administration of Parliament under the Parliamentary Commission. There is a general feeling among other staff that the PBO is a 'super department' because it has better facilities, including offices, office equipment and vehicles. These are the facilities which were initially provided by donors to the PBO at the time of inception. The fact that the funds under some economic management projects are directed specifically to the PBO also did not auger well with other officials in the Parliamentary Commission. The bureaucracy in the administration of Parliament sometime causes delays to the PBO's work. The time spent between requisitioning and release of funds for office accessories (even small ones including papers, toner, fuel and so on) bogs down the PBO's work.

(v)   **Demands from members of parliament:** Members of parliament by their very nature (generally) do not like reading, especially big reports with figures. The PBO puts in a lot of work but only a few MPs utilize the reports. MPs are always demanding information which has already been provided to them previously, some even expect information to be collected for them for individual private projects. The PBO sometimes finds itself overwhelmed by MPs' demands; though the requirement of requesting information should be through the Budget Committee or clerk to Parliament, some MPs do not follow this procedure.

Conclusions: lessons for other parliaments

Legislatures in different counties have different traditions regarding their level of participation in the budget-formulation process. The need for as much participation as possible cannot be overemphasized as the budget is the single most important tool through which economic and social policy can be influenced. With more participation, parliaments will be in better a position to play their three basic roles of representation, legislation (law-making) and financial and physical oversight.

The executive will not facilitate parliaments to participate more in the budget formulation; this means that parliaments, especially in Africa and other developing economies, should be facilitated to initiate their own legislation that will ensure for them this participation.

There is a need to share experiences and assist in building capacity in other parliaments to make them more effective in ensuring better public policies and more prudent management of public resources. Parliaments will need to be assisted with funds, personnel and initial office equipment as well as capacity to utilize the private members' bills and lobbying skills to bring onboard colleagues and non-governmental bodies, including civil society organizations, to garner support for more transparent budgeting.

The establishment of Uganda's Parliamentary Budget Office and its successes and challenges offer a lot of lessons for other parliaments. Experts in the Ugandan Parliamentary Budget Office are happy to share these experiences with other parliaments in need.

Note

1   USAID = United States Agency for International Development; DfID = Department for International Development (United Kingdom); GTZ = Deutsche Gesellschaft für Internationale Zusammenarbeit; EU = European Union; NORAD = Norwegian Agency for Development Cooperation.

4   Promoting gender equality in the Tanzanian Parliament

Anne Makinda

Perhaps the greatest reform that the Tanzanian National Assembly – or Bunge – has seen in recent years is the remarkable increase in the number of female members of parliament (MPs). Tanzania has made a big step forward on gender equality, and is ahead of many African countries. To address the severe gender gap in parliamentary representation the Tanzanian Parliament changed the Constitution to install a gender quota system, also known as the special-seat system or the reserved-seat system for women. The quota system is meant to enhance the rights and opportunities of women, and aims to improve their electoral performance, strengthen their participation within political parties and boost their representation in Parliament. Currently, there are 83 women MPs in the Tanzanian Parliament, approximately 23 per cent of the total number of MPs. Seventy-five of these came through affirmative action, five were appointed by the president and two are from the House of Representatives of Zanzibar.

Tanzania has adopted the quota system as a strategy for Parliament to counter the numerous negative factors that affect women's participation in politics. The main obstacles facing women in politics are a lack of finances, a related lack of education and training, and cultural barriers. The role women are expected to play in Tanzanian society is the one of wives and mothers; politics is considered not to be a female domain. Women in Tanzania only received the right to vote and stand for elections in 1959, and have traditionally won only a small portion of regular (constituency)[1] seats. However, like in most African countries, women are not able to compete for elective office due to the existing obstacles. Even if women decide to run for election, they are subject to threats, insults and sexual harassment during their campaigns. Special seats can avoid that and improve gender balance in the legislature.

The history of women's representation in Parliament

The political will on the part of the governments in power to increase women's representation in parliament has been immensely influential to achieve this goal. Our first President, Mr. Nyerere, was supported by strong and influential women in his fight for Tanzanian independence, and consistently advocated for greater women's representation within the government and his political party. The Chama cha Mapinduzi (CCM) constitution specifically addresses equal opportunities to all citizens, women and men, irrespective of colour, tribe or religion. Women within the CCM have traditionally spoken out for more women in politics. 'Special' seats in the Tanzanian Parliament were created at independence to ensure representation of diverse groups, which included women. Despite this, the number of women in parliament was negligible: the number of female 'constituency' MPs had never exceeded five, and was even zero for the period 1980 from 1985. The percentage of women in Parliament through constituency elections declined from 7.5 per cent from 1961 to 1965 to 3 per cent from 1970 to 1975. The reality did not match Nyerere's and CCM's beliefs on gender equality. It was decided that the system then in place to ensure gender balance in politics was not sufficient as it did not guarantee a certain number or percentage of parliamentary seats for women. The social and economic disadvantages of women were such that a quota system was needed to guarantee representation of women in the Parliament. CCM designed the quota system to overcome society's negative perceptions about women in politics and the quota system made sure the number of female MPs was both greater and more predictable.

The quota system was first introduced in 1985. Special-seat MPs perform the same functions as constituency MPs. In Parliament they participate in debates, they serve on parliamentary committees, and vote on bills. Outside of Parliament they run various projects. However, the representation function of special-seat MPs is broader than that of a constituency MP, because special-seat MPs serve a region, which consists of four to nine constituencies.

Unlike constituency MPs, special-seat MPs are indirectly elected. During the period of single-party rule, candidates were elected by constituency members in the National Assembly among nominees submitted by the National Executive Committee of CCM. At that time 15 seats were reserved for women and another 15 seats were reserved for mass organizations affiliated to CCM, such as youth organizations, workers organizations, parental organizations, and the Union of Tanzanian Women (UWT). Thus, women could win special seats through 15 seats allocated for women, through UWT, or through other mass organizations. There had to be at least one woman represented from each region, as well as representation from the other minority organizations.

For the 1995 election, the Eighth Constitutional Amendment in 1992 (which also marks the political transition to multi-party rule) replaced 15 special seats with a new total, defined as 15 per cent of the Tanzanian House of Representatives, and it abolished the special seats representing other organizations. The Eighth Amendment also changed the election procedure for special seats, and for the past 2 legislatures (from 1995 to 2000 and from 2000 to 2005) special seats were distributed proportionally on the basis of the number of votes won by each party in the parliamentary election, not on the basis of the number of parliamentary seats won by each party. Only parties that won at least 5 per cent of all valid votes in a parliamentary election can propose the names of special-seat candidates to the National Electoral Commission.

The political parties have used internal mechanisms to nominate special-seat candidates, as they have for constituency seats. With respect to CCM, aspirants – who should be members of the Union of Tanzanian Women (UWT), the women's wing of CCM – submit their application forms to district offices of the UWT. UWT district offices then forward the names to the UWT regional conferences, which consist of UWT leaders and female leaders from wards, districts, and regions, for contest. Each regional conference forwards the names of the top 5 aspirants to the UWT national congress, which prioritizes and nominates candidates, who need to be approved by the National Executive Committee of the CCM. Although at a national level Tanzania has a first-pass-the-post system, special seats for women within the CCM are elected through proportional representation. The CCM's nomination procedure for special seats is very competitive, and aspirants campaign hard to be selected at each level of screening. Competition is very fierce, so the women that are chosen tend to be highly qualified.

Even though the parliamentary elections in 1995 saw an increase of 13 per cent in representation of women in the Bunge, this was deemed insufficient. The Thirteenth Constitutional Amendment in 2000 raised the proportion of special seats to 20 per cent for the 2000 election and 30 per cent in 2005. The increase in percentages can be attributed to the lobbying efforts of UWT, women politicians, and political will on the part of the government to enhance women's political representation.

There is now 30.4 per cent representation of women in the Parliament. Now, the Parliament is unicameral with a total of 323 seats. Two hundred and thirty two members are elected by direct popular vote in single-member constituencies using the first-past-the-post system; 75 seats are reserved for women elected by their political parties on the basis of proportional representation; five members are indirectly elected by the Zanzibar House of Representatives; up to 10 members may be appointed by the president; and one seat is reserved for the attorney general. Members serve five-year terms. Today, of the 10 positions appointed by the president, half are women. Without a quota system women would only account for 7 per cent of seats in Parliament, given the fact that only 17 women were elected to represent constituencies in the latest legislative election of 2005.

A stepping stone to constituency seats

There has been criticism regarding the usefulness of the special-seat system, and questions have emerged on the further use of the system. Some say the increase in the number of women in Parliament is a form of 'window dressing', rather than a way to engender Tanzanian society. The special-seat system for women was born as a temporary gap-filling strategy, meant to be revoked when women's socio-economic conditions improved and women gained more political experience. Special seats were meant to serve as a stepping stone to constituency seats, and the Tanzanian experience shows that they do in fact serve as a springboard for more prominent political careers for women.

Most female MPs have entered the legislature through the special-seat system. Special seats provide an easier way to get into Parliament, in light of the cultural and resources barriers women face. This is why sometimes experienced MPs continued to seek special seats. This doesn't mean that those women are not 'electable'. Competition for special seats is harsh, so the women that are chosen tend to be highly qualified. Special seats have been the major path for women to Parliament, but the number of women elected in constituencies has also increased. Only four women were elected in constituencies when the special-seat system for women was established in 1985, but seventeen were elected in constituencies in 2005. A majority of women elected in constituencies in 1995 and 2000 started their parliamentary career as a special-seat MP.

The number of female constituency candidates has increased over time. On the one hand this is due to training and capacity building of women that want to serve in politics. Several women's NGOs such as the Tanzania Gender Networking Program encourage women to stand for constituency seats and offer seminars, symposia, forums and workshops to train female aspirants in confidence building, public speaking, campaign management, fundraising, lobbying and leadership. They also urge political parties to nominate more women. There is also a women's caucus within Parliament, the Tanzanian Women Parliamentary Group (TWPG), of which I am the chairperson. The caucus was formed in 1992 and because women's issues go beyond party lines, the caucus is non-partisan. Drawing its members from sitting female MPs, TWPG was created to improve coordination among them regarding women's issues, and to empower female MPs. The caucus meets with each session of Parliament. After elections the women's caucus trains the new female MPs, both on special and constituency seats, on how to debate and ask questions in Parliament. We tell female ministers when they give a wrong answer to a question from Parliament, and we let them know if there are any other complaints. To improve MPs' performance and to prepare them for real-life parliamentary debates, we organize a 'model' parliament where women can practice their skills. The caucus has been very instrumental in encouraging special-seat MPs to run for constituency seats, providing them with advice and training, including mental training for the challenges that female candidates usually encounter during their campaigns in the constituencies. The caucus tries to initiate projects in the country as well. For example, just recently the 'Tanzania Women's Bank' was founded. The Bank lends money to women who want to start profitable projects. Female MPs are the main shareholders, and they are the ones who provided the start-up capital.

On the other hand, the increase in constituency seats for women reflects an increased awareness of the electorate regarding the benefits of having female MPs. Norms and values are slowly beginning to change because of the good track record most special-seat and female constituency MPs have. They are strong women who serve as role models for the women of Africa.

My own struggle for political representation and for gender recognition is typical. In 1975 I became active in national politics when I was nominated to be an MP through the CCM youth seat. At that time it was still one-party rule, and there was a system in place of having MPs from various backgrounds, such as those who were parents, women, those from universities and youth. I got the opportunity to enter the legislature through the latter, and I have been a member of parliament ever since. I have been on the special youth seat until 1995, when I became a constituency MP for Njombe South.

Although I had experience competing for the special youth seat within CCM, the first time I ran for constituency elections was a very negative and exhausting experience for me. The race was between me and a male competitor. He was trying to win votes by using Tanzania's prejudice against women in leadership positions. He embarrassed me in public, and told the women in my constituency that if they voted for me, I would castrate their men. At one point, even my own church was against me. I am used to being part of the minority; when I studied there were two women and 56 men, when I was regional governor I was the only woman out of 25 positions. Because of misunderstandings and cultural barriers, men often accuse me of arguing against them. My strategy is always to confront and debate, which is what I did when I ran for elections. I won only with a very minimal difference in votes. Even though I had occupied ministerial positions for many years the electorate's cultural bias against women almost brought me down. But the story did not finish there. Because my opponent did not want to accept his loss against a woman, he took me to the highest court in the country to fight against the election outcome. It took four years before the tiring lawsuit was finally over, but I won the court case. In the 2000 elections we competed against each other again. I won those elections too, and have been a constituency MP for Njombe South ever since. It shows that voters are willing to re-elect female constituency MPs with a proven track record.

The benefits of female representation

There has been a big impact of women MPs on the issues discussed in Parliament. Women are very vocal in Parliament and because of their role in society women are aware of issues that men are not, especially with regard to children and women issues. As a result, women MPs have been able to push for laws that address women's needs in several areas: there is now maternity leave for both married and unmarried mothers; female candidates are now allowed to enter university directly after high school; there is increased severity of punishment of sexual offenders; customary practices that discriminated against women with regard to land ownership have been declared unconstitutional; 'priority to the girl child' is now the new motto, with the result that pregnant girls can now continue going to school. Besides gender-specific issues, women MPs also fight more for water and sanitation facilities than their male counterparts. Efforts have been made by Parliament to monitor the national budget to ensure that women's concerns are taken into account, to ensure that gender issues are incorporated into the formulation and implementation of policy and laws.

The requirement now is that in every ministry there should be a gender committee. The Ministry of Community Development, Women Affairs and Children ensures the implementation of gender policy and organizes workshops countrywide and distributes brochures to create public awareness on the importance of gender equality.

Don't get me wrong, I am not an MP for women only. I am an MP for all people in my constituency. However, it is my strong belief that the development of Tanzania will accelerate when women have better access to water, education and an income. I think that women cannot be relieved from poverty if no-one stands up for them. When I visit my constituency I like to stay and sleep in the villages to be amongst my people. At night, everyone gets together and we can talk about important issues. It was at one of those occasions that the men and women apologized to me for allowing the behaviour of my election competitor to continue. They told me their perception of women in charge had changed over the years. That was a very gratifying moment for me. Right now, my district has the highest HIV/AIDS rate in the country. Unfortunately the disease is more prominent in women than men. I campaigned hard to make sure everybody went to get tested, so now we have a clear overview of who is infected and who is not and we can target further action to that information. I am also currently working on building schools and providing water to all my constituents. The situation is difficult for women who have not gone to school, because they are pinned down by customs and traditions. That's why we insist on educating the girl child. It is through education that women can truly be liberated. I am also trying to improve women's access to capital so that they can provide their own income. Women's access to credit is still difficult due to collateral requirements.

Because in Tanzania we are dealing with extremely poor people, I pay for a lot of goods and services for my constituents out of my own pocket if I'm asked for my help. For instance, women do not go to court in Tanzania. That is in part caused by the fact that they wouldn't know what to say and in part because they don't have the money to cover the costs. So I try to stimulate them and I sometimes pay for their court fees. I also work closely together with the church, and the pastor discusses my plans in his service. I try to be as generous with my time, energy and material resources as possible. I teach women not to sit down and think that men are the reason for their underdevelopment. It is tough being a female MP, but in the end I enjoy it because I can really make a difference.

Female representation within the Southern African Development Community (SADC) region

In 1997 the Tanzanian government signed the SADC-PF Declaration by Heads of State or Government on Gender and Development which called for 'equal representation of women and men in the decision making of member states and SADC structures at all levels, and the achievement of at least 30 per cent target of women in political and decision making structures by year 2005'. Tanzania is one of a handful of countries that meet the 30 per cent target, along with South Africa, Mozambique, Rwanda and Burundi. Unlike South Africa and Mozambique, Tanzania has a national first-pass-the-post system, which makes it more difficult for women to win elections than it is under a system of proportional representation. Only Tanzania has proceeded to legislate the inclusion of women in parliament and has gone ahead to create quotas. The Tanzanian Parliament is becoming a force to be reckoned with in the region, especially in its far-reaching reforms to achieve gender equality. With a goal of 50:50 parity for 2020 and with its current 30.4 per cent female representation, the Parliament is among the world leaders in this area of gender balance in politics.

Although some countries in the region are doing very well in promoting gender representation, others are less advanced in accomplishing equality between men and women. Let me illustrate this with two examples. First, in 2003 the Parliamentary Centre initiated a working group on poverty reduction for African MPs. The working group brings together MPs from South, East and West Africa. I serve on the executive committee, and we are appointing new committee members this year. Each region nominates two people for the executive committee, while taking into account gender balance. To my surprise the proposed candidates were mostly men, and gender equality proved not to be taken seriously. Even the women didn't think it was a problem that there were going to be significantly more men than women serving on the committee. It breaks my heart to witness this type of attitude. I am going to lobby and use the working group's newsletter to explain why we shouldn't compromise our gender principles. Second, Botswana, which doesn't have a quota system, elected only two female MPs (out of fifty-seven) in its last election in 2009. These are just some examples that show that not all over Africa norms as to how we view women have changed.

To help promote gender equality in politics, the Tanzanian women's caucus has helped countries within the SADC region to start their own caucus. Zambia, Mozambique and Malawi now have similar women's discussion groups. Before, the women in those countries were not even talking to each other or sharing their experiences. There is now also an SADC regional women's caucus, which gets together twice a year. The regional caucus discusses advocacy within countries, and provides capacity building for female MPs. Such networks ensure that information is circulating, that initiatives are catching on and opinions are changing.

Future

Tanzania is determined to attain gender parity of 50 per cent in all spheres of life and at all levels of political decision-making positions, including Parliament, by the year 2020. This goal was integrated in the 2010 election manifesto. In Tanzania, the issue has been tabled in party caucuses and it is now before the central committee of Parliament. Various methods, including capacity building, advocacy on the ground and within the party, and a further increase in the percentage of parliamentary seats for women from 30 per cent have been discussed as ways for achieving these gender objectives. For instance, the women's caucus and the CCM are encouraging women that occupy special seats to move on to constituency seats and to open up their spot up for other women. We are also trying to influence the (often male) political (party) leaders on nominating and identifying women that could run for special seats and/or constituency seats in the next election. We then help these women prepare election material, and we give them practical tips on how to go out and campaign.

The Millennium Development Goals also play a role in our future gender policies. A significant decrease in maternal mortality has to be achieved before 2015, although pregnancy-related deaths continue to be a major threat to women in Tanzania. I have suggested the organization of bigger training events for all MPs to sensitize lawmakers on their role in the prevention of maternal deaths with the goal of achieving the MDG target in the upcoming years.

Women MPs have to continue to serve as role models for other women, and that's what they are doing. The women in politics in Tanzania are strong women, each fighting against poverty for their people. For instance, Anne Kilango Malecesa, who is a constituency MP for Same East and used to be on a special women's seat, was given an award by the US government for being an outstanding woman in fighting corruption. What matters is for the people, both men and women, to understand their roles and responsibilities in their own development. The world is about fighting for individual and collective rights. Working together is crucial, as only then will everyone recognize women as a vital force in our countries' development. To achieve this, women have to support one another. We have to stand as one.

Note

1 'Constituency' MPs being those elected by citizens at large, in regular constituencies (as opposed to 'reserve' or 'special-seat' MPs).

5 Peace-building and national reconciliation
The role of the Rwandan Parliament

Joseph Karemera

Background

Rwanda has existed as a nation-state since the eleventh century. Contrary to popular belief, Rwanda has not historically been divided along the ethnic lines of the Hutu, Tutsi and Twa. In fact it was under Belgian rule (1916–1962) that a deliberate policy of divide and rule, aimed at establishing and entrenching the notion of racial differences, was first pursued. The consequence of this policy was that Rwanda entered the post-colonial era weighed down by an ideology that emphasized ethnic divisions. As a consequence, between 1959 and 1994, the political elite in Rwanda was primarily focused on manipulating ethnic tensions in order to obtain/remain in power as opposed to concerning itself with promoting the welfare of the population at large.

The increasingly ethnically motivated and divisive nature of politics, coupled with the neglect of a developmental agenda resulted in escalating inter-community violence and culminated in the 1994 genocide which saw up to a million Tutsi lose their lives. Yet, despite these traumatic events the Rwandan people were able to begin a process of civil reconciliation that enabled the country to avoid becoming a permanent failed state. This chapter outlines how this remarkable task of reconciliation was accomplished and, more specifically, the role that the new, post-1994, parliament played in this effort.

A brief history of the state of affairs before the genocide

Racial tensions in Rwanda were significantly exacerbated following a 1973 coup carried out by Habyalimana and his allies against the First Republic. This was because, even though both the coup leaders and the civilian government they replaced were Hutu, the new regime consisted of ethnic Hutus from the north of the country as opposed to the leadership of the First Republic, which mainly hailed from the south and central regions. The new military regime exacerbated tensions by: (1) killing the remnants of the Tutsi elite; and (2) discriminating and even killing Hutus from the south and central regions. Thus, the actions of the new regime (Second Republic) had the effect of generating new intra-Hutu mistrust and hatred, further undermining any notion of Rwandan unity.

The Liberation War and the genocide against the Tutsi (1990–1994)

In 1990 the exiled Rwandese Patriotic Front (RPF) began waging a liberation war against the one-party dictatorship of the Second Republic. This conflict resulted in the escalation of crimes and the violation of the human rights of the Tutsi minority as well as moderate Hutus. Furthermore, this conflict was deceitfully manipulated by the leaders of the dictatorship who managed to portray the war as an attack against a Hutu regime by the Tutsi. The government was able to exploit this fear through propaganda generated to begin a countrywide mobilization of Hutu militia with the stated objective of executing a full-scale extermination of the remaining Tutsi and moderate Hutus. The genocide peaked during a 90-day period in 1994. By the end of the genocide up to a million Tutsi had been murdered. The genocide dealt a knockout blow to the already ailing peace and unity amongst the Rwandese, with the country virtually becoming a failed state.

The role of the Rwandan Parliament in peace-building and reconciliation

Given the legacy of racial division and the loss of legitimacy suffered by the country's political institutions owing to the genocide, peace-building and national reconciliation was not going to be an easy task. A central mechanism in achieving cross-community reconciliation was to ensure that the new political institutions that would emerge were representative of the population of the country with respect to ethnicity, sex and disability, as well as different age groups. Obviously, given the central role of the legislature in ensuring: (1) the representation of citizens; and (2) the exercise of executive oversight, the new Rwandan Parliament needed to be at the forefront of the reconciliation process if this was to be successful.

Specifically, Parliament's contribution to national reconciliation can be subdivided into two distinct phases:

1   The transition period (July 1994 to 2003), that is the period immediately after the genocide, when governance institutions were less legitimate and inter-ethnic division, tension and mistrust were at a climax.
2   Post transition (2003 to the present), when governance institutions were legitimate and calm had essentially returned to the country.

The Broad Base Transitional Parliament (BBTP) in the transition period – post genocide (1994–2003)

After stopping the genocide, the RPF invited political parties that had not participated in the genocide to form a transitional government of national unity commonly referred to as the Broad Base Transitional Government (BBTG). As part of this process, on 25 November 1994, the Broad Base Transitional Parliament (BBTP) was put in place as one of the institutions of this unity government. Unlike any other parliament in the history of the country, it was composed of representatives from eight political parties. The BBTP operated under the rules of the Fundamental Law that was established after the 1994 genocide. The Fundamental Law enshrined the following principals: (1) the rule of law; (2) multi-party politics and power sharing; (3) the unconditional repatriation of refugees; (4) the establishment of a national reconciliation commission; and (5) a protocol on commitment to respect human rights.

Composition and structure

The BBTP was composed of seventy members. Parties were represented in accordance with the principles of the Fundamental Law. Specifically, four major parties each contributed thirteen members of parliament; one party and the army each contributed six members; while three smaller parties each contributed two members. Later in the transition period it was decided that the national youth and women's organizations should be represented in the BBTP. Subsequently, each one of these organizations nominated two representatives. Thus, in the end the BBTP had seventy-four members. Each individual nominated by a party only became a member of parliament following scrutiny by an all-party conference – a process put in place in order to ensure that individuals involved in the genocide were not able to undermine the legitimacy and effectiveness of the BBTP.

The structure of the BBTP was similar to that of parliaments in neighbouring countries. It included the following organs:

1   The Parliament was headed by a Speaker belonging to one of the major parties (the Social Democratic Party (PSD)) and deputized by a Deputy Speaker from another major party (the Liberal Party (PL)) while a member of one of the smaller parties headed the Parliamentary Bureau. Furthermore, the Parliamentary Bureau was itself assisted by parliamentary services headed by the Clerk of Parliament.
2   The Plenary Assembly was the supreme organ of the Parliament and was composed of all its members.
3   The Conference of the Chairpersons was another important institution and was composed of the chairpersons and vice-chairpersons of all the standing committees in Parliament and the Parliamentary Bureau. The aim of the Conference was to ensure that Parliament's strategic plans of action were being implemented.
4   The inclusive power sharing fostered by this modus operandi had a reassuring effect amongst politicians and the people as it instilled a sense of ownership, of the governance process, to all segments of society. The RPF, which was a leading party, won the confidence of most politicians and the general population because it did not monopolize power after defeating the murderous regime of the Second Republic single-handed. This was a welcome surprise, but most importantly a major shift in the governance history of Rwanda.

Functioning

The BBTP's task was essentially threefold: (1) legislation; (2) oversight of the executive; and (3) representation of the population.

LEGISLATIVE FUNCTIONS TO ENHANCE RECONCILIATION

The BBTP embarked on passing laws which addressed issues of peace-building and reconciliation. But, most importantly, the BBTP ensured that the rule of law and other principles enshrined in the Fundamental Law were observed and adhered to by all parties. The BBTP also enacted laws establishing institutions that helped to promote unity and reconciliation as well as effective governance. This included legislating to create:

1   Institutions designed to promote reconciliation: such as: (1) The National Reconciliation Commission (NRC), a body established to deal exclusively with reconciliation activities on a day-to-day basis; (2) The National Human Rights Commission (NHRC), a body established to promote human rights; (3) The Fonds d'Assistance aux Rescap{ea}s du Genocide (FARG), a fund that was established to assist survivors of the genocide to meet essential needs such as medical treatment, building a house, schooling of genocide orphans and so on. The law stipulated that 5 per cent of the national budget has to be devoted to this fund.
2   Institutions designed to promote efficiency and good governance, such as the Office of the Auditor General. An institution established to evaluate how the government used its financial resources and thus providing specialist information, to Parliament, in order to assist it in its oversight functions.

OVERSIGHT OF THE EXECUTIVE WITH RESPECT TO ISSUES OF UNITY
AND RECONCILIATION

The Parliament carried out its executive oversight functions through the use of relevant standing committees. These committees also played a vital role in ensuring that budgets for reconciliation activities were given special attention in order to facilitate the national healing process.

OTHER PARLIAMENTARY ACTIVITIES TO ENHANCE RECONCILIATION

Parliamentarians played a pivotal role in mobilizing the population in order to facilitate national unity and reconciliation. This contribution was achieved via an outreach programme carried out by all members of parliament. Specifically, members of parliament actively participated as resource persons in national reconciliation and peace-building programmes in military units and reintegration centres for retuning soldiers from the DR Congo and refugees.

The parliamentarians also engaged with their peers from the other countries in the Great Lakes Region, actively working towards peace-building in the region and paying particular attention to information dissemination regarding genocide ideology. This task was achieved directly through parliament-to-parliament engagement and also through regional parliamentary organizations like the AMANI FORUM in which Rwandan parliamentarians have been quite active.

Setting the stage to exit the period of transition and reforming Parliament

In 1998 the RPF-led government organized a national consultative forum. The objective of this forum was to prepare for how and when Rwanda could exit the transition period. The forum consisted of cabinet ministers, members of parliament, academics, senior political party executives and veteran politicians, church leaders and other members of civil society as well as leaders from sub-national government. Experts in relevant fields were also invited to contribute to the process in the areas of their expertise.

The consultation took almost two years and reached the conclusion that Rwanda's new constitution should enshrine the following principals: (1) sovereignty of the people; (2) political pluralism; (3) the separation of powers; and (4) the rule of law. In concrete terms these aspirations were manifest in the ways in which the constitution would guarantee (1) that executive power should be dispersed; (2) the adoption of a proportional representation electoral system; and (3) that special attention and emphasis should be paid to fundamental human rights.

The new constitution

In 2000, after the national consultations exercises were concluded, the government appointed a twelve-member constitutional commission. The commission was comprised of representatives of political parties, civil society and independent experts. The commission's stated objective was to produce a new constitution after an extensive public consultation.

The new Constitution formally incorporated the principles emphasized by the National Consultation Forum. The principle of consensus politics became a constitutional reality via Article 116 of the Constitution, which states that no matter which party wins an election it cannot have more than 50 per cent of cabinet seats. The Constitution also enshrined pluralism by stipulating that: (1) the President of the Republic and the Speaker of the Chamber of Deputies must belong to different political parties (Article 58); (2) members of parliament cannot be cabinet members (Article 68); and (3) 30 per cent of decision-making roles must be allocated to women.

The Constitution also established the Forum for Political Parties, whose leadership rotates amongst its members. The objective of the Political Party Forum is to provide a means for cross-party consultation on major issues facing the country, generating new policy proposals, mediating in conflicts between political organizations, and assisting in resolving conflicts within a given political party on request of the said party.

Parliamentary reform

The 2003 Constitution reformed the Parliament of Rwanda in order to further deepen the gains made in the long transition period.

Structure

The new Constitution introduced a bicameral legislative structure with the new Parliament consisting of two separate houses: (1) the Senate (upper house) and (2) the Chamber of Deputies (lower house). The internal structures of both Houses are similar. Specifically each chamber has:

1   A Plenary Assembly, which is the supreme organ and composed of all members of each house.
2   A Bureau, composed, in the case of the Senate, of the President of the Senate and the two Vice-Presidents, and, in the case of the Chamber of Deputies, of the Speaker and the two Vice-Speakers. In both chambers the three members of the bureau come from three different political parties and at least one has to be a woman. Each Vice-President or Vice-Speaker has a different role in the bureau, one follows up parliamentary affairs and another follow up administration and financial affairs for the purposes of informing both the bureau and the Conference of Chairpersons (see below).
3   A Conference of Chairpersons, composed of the members of the Bureau and the chairpersons and vice-chairpersons of all standing committees of each chamber.
4   A disciplinary committee that checks on the discipline of members and also evaluates the overall performance of each chamber with respect to whether it is fulfilling all of its legal obligations.

Composition

The Senate has twenty-six members (Article 82) who enjoy an eight-year non-renewable term. Members of the Senate are elected or nominated objectively on individual merit without regard to political affiliation as follows: twelve members are elected by regional councils in accordance with administrative jurisdictions, four are appointed by the Forum of Political Organisation; one member is elected by public university academic and research staff, one member is elected by private university academic research staff and eight are nominated by the president of the Republic, who has to ensure that historically marginalized community interests are taken into consideration when making appointments (Article 82). Former heads of state who honourably completed their term of office become members of the Senate by submitting a request to the Supreme Court.

On the other hand, the Chamber of Deputies has eighty members, elected as follows (Articles 76 and 77): 53 members are elected by direct universal suffrage from a final list of names using a system of proportional representation. The rest of the seats are allocated to the political parties based on the number of votes received at the election and in accordance with the system of highest surplus. It is worth noting that the party lists must reflect the principle of national unity and gender equality (Articles 9 and 54) of the 2003 Constitution. Consequently, twenty-four women are elected by specific women councils in accordance to state administrative entities; two deputies are elected by the national youth council; and the national federation of the disabled people elects one deputy, who must be a disabled member, to represent them in the chamber of deputies.

Mission

The mission of the Rwandan Parliament is expected to perform includes supervision of fundamental principles enshrined in the 2003 Constitution. Those principles include:

1 Fighting the ideology of genocide and all its manifestations;
2 Eradication of ethnic, regional and other divisions and promotion of national unity;
3 Equitable sharing of power;
4 Building a state governed by: (1) the rule of law, (2) a pluralistic democratic government that guarantees the equality of all Rwandans and equality between women and men;
5 Building a state committed to promoting social welfare and establishing appropriate mechanisms for ensuring social justice;
6 The constant quest for solutions through dialogue and consensus;

7   Prohibiting political organizations from promoting sectarian policies based on discrimination with respect to race, ethnicity, tribal affiliation, clans, religion or any policy that results in discrimination.
8   Ensure that political organizations reflect the unity of the people of Rwanda.

In addition to these general functions the Senate carries out in-depth research on the fundamental principles stipulated in Articles 9 and 54 of the Constitution. Findings are published and become the basis for policy revision. This clearly gives Parliament the role of ensuring that national reconciliation actually happens. The other specific responsibilities of the Senate include responsibility for approving senior appointments made by the president of the Republic or the prime minister (Article 88), including:

1   the president, the vice-president of the Supreme Court, the prosecutor general of the Republic and his or her deputy;
2   chairpersons and members of national commissions;
3   ombudsman and their deputies;
4   the auditor-general and his or her deputy;
5   ambassadors and representatives to international organisations;
6   provincial governors and heads of public enterprises, which have legal personality.

The Senate also follows up elections in the country. It produces two reports on any election, one regarding the preparation of elections and the second immediately after the election. The preelection report assesses the adequacy of the preparation effort, identifying if anything needs to be corrected in order to ensure free and fair elections. The Electoral Commission is legally obliged to comply with the Senate's recommendations. The post-election report indicates how free and fair the election was, providing potential lessons for the future.

Legislation

The Chamber of Deputies scrutinizes and votes on all the bills originating from the executive or private members. The bills that survive scrutiny are sent to the Senate for review and voting on by the Senate before being returned to the Chamber of Deputies. In accordance with the Constitution (Article 88), the Senate is only competent to vote on the following laws:

1   All organic laws.
2   Laws relating to: (1) amendments to the constitution; (2) defence and security; (3) public enterprises; (4) para-state organizations and (5) territorial organizations.
3   Changes in: (1) the criminal law; (2) laws relating to the jurisdiction of courts and; (3) laws relating to procedures in criminal cases, fundamental freedoms, rights as well as laws relating to elections, referenda and international agreements and treaties.
4   In the event the Senate (1) does not approve a bill forwarded to it or (2) the amendments to a bill it proposed are not acceptable to the Chamber of Deputies, both chambers set up a joint committee composed of an equal number of deputies and senators which examines the bill and makes proposals on how to resolve the deadlock. In case the compromise generated by the committee is not adopted by both chambers, the bill is returned to its initiator.

The Senate's legislative role is limited as:

1   The Senate does not vote on the financial bill, it only scrutinises it and gives its opinion to the chamber of deputies before they vote on it.
2   Initiation of bills is the exclusive work of the Chamber of Deputies and the executive. The Senate only initiates the organic law on the Senate's rules of procedure.

Oversight

The two chambers carry out oversight on the activities of the executive independent of each other. They do so at all levels of government and in all public departments.

When an oversight mechanism is to be utilized the Speaker or the President of the Senate informs the prime minister of the event. The prime minister normally sends the relevant minister unless the oversight pertains to a cross-cutting issue or concerns more than one ministry; in which case (s)he attends in person.

The mechanisms used for oversight include: oral questions, written questions, committee hearings, commissions of inquiry, open questioning in plenary session and, in the case of the Chamber of Deputies, a motion of no confidence can be made. The Senate can carry out a commission of inquiry but cannot move a vote of no confidence. Hearings are carried out publically and in most cases reported live on the day's television news.

The important relationship between the executive and Parliament

The president of the Republic, after consultation with the Speaker of the Chamber of Deputies, the President of the Senate, the prime minister and the president of the Supreme Court, can dissolve the Chamber of Deputies if the interests of the country are in jeopardy. This can happen only once in his term of office. The Senate shall not be dissolved under any circumstance (Article 133).

The prime minister informs both chambers of Parliament about government activities quarterly at a joint sitting. He or she communicates to both bureaus the contents of cabinet meetings and decisions made, not later than eight days after a cabinet meeting has taken place (Article 134).

Challenges in peace-building and national reconciliation

Despite the progress made, a number of challenges remain if Rwanda is to achieve its goal of eliminating inter-group tensions. These challenges include:

1 The fact that some individuals, especially morally bankrupt politicians, continue to attempt to promote ethnic differences.
2 Despite recent socio-economic development, the existence of chronic poverty and ignorance amongst large segments of the population continue to make people vulnerable to political manipulations.
3 The proximity of genocide survivors and perpetrators generates inter-community mistrust, especially when some perpetrators attempt to kill survivors in order to destroy evidence of their crimes.
4 Reparation that is difficult to obtain because of the economic circumstances of the perpetrators can result in feelings of resentment amongst victims.

Opportunities

Despite the above-mentioned challenges there are some important opportunities that can continue to be leveraged in order to further enhance peace-building and the national reconciliation effort. They include:

1 Political leadership: the rapid change in politics following the genocide was possible because of a very strong commitment,

from the top political leadership of Rwanda, to revive the nation. Specifically, President Paul Kagame and his ruling party, the Rwandese Patriotic Front, were instrumental in facilitating reconciliation by initiating the process of power sharing amongst different groups in society. This positive influence did not take long to percolate to the rest of the country's leadership and to the population in general.

2   Relations amongst the Rwandese: efforts to build bridges between communities as well as making people aware of the commonalities of the people of Rwanda, including their shared heritage, should be an effective means of combating the legacy of ethnic divisions.

3   Ensuring the functioning of the highly representative model of democracy enshrined in the new Constitution is accompanied by socio-economic development and equality of opportunity for all. Thus, fostering both political inclusion and the possibility of individual betterment.

Conclusion

Following the tragic events of 1994, effective reconciliation and peace-building efforts in Rwanda needed to address the root causes of disunity. Given the central role of Parliament in both representing the people and facilitating the good governance and development required to foster such reconciliation it was critical that a functional Rwandese Parliament be established. Both the BBTP and the post-2003 parliament were able to contribute to this national goal. This was because: (1) their broad-based representation provided a means by which every group in the country could feel that they had a stake in the reconstruction project; and (2) by ensuring the oversight of the executive, the Parliament managed to facilitate the effective channelling of resources towards reconstruction and development. Thus, by directly addressing, and to some extent ameliorating, the toxic ethnic-based political legacy and neglect of good governance that had existed prior to 1994, the Rwandan Parliaments have played a critical role in the national healing process.

6   Reaching out to citizens
Enhancing the opportunity for private members bills and creating constituency offices in Zambia

Given Lubinda

In 1991 Zambia changed its system of governance from a single-party state to multi-party democracy. The National Assembly of Zambia developed a parliamentary reform programme and, with the 2002 elections –as a result of which opposition parties gained a small majority in Parliament – reforms gathered momentum. In this Chapter, I present two important areas of reform: (i) revision to the rules and procedures of Parliament (the Standing Orders); and (ii) the outreach by Parliament to citizens, through the creation of constituency offices.

Background

Following the introduction of multi-party democracy, the National Assembly of Zambia found it prudent to realign its functions with the demands of plural politics. This called for the introduction of parliamentary reforms with a view to addressing some of the limitations which existed in the institution at that time.

The National Assembly of Zambia and a Parliamentary Working Group of Donors joined efforts in November 2002 to support a programme of parliamentary reform, funded by the United States Agency for International Development. The reform programme was conceived in order to enhance parliamentary oversight of the activities of the executive and also to allow for increased participation of the citizens in the affairs of the country. It worked towards increased interface, interaction, communication and consultation between members of parliament (MPs) and their constituents and between the National Assembly and the general public, thereby bringing Parliament closer to the people.

The reforms were started by the signing of a memorandum of understanding between the National Assembly and the cooperating partners comprising Canada, Ireland, Sweden, the Netherlands and the United States. The National Assembly established a Parliamentary Reforms and Modernisation Committee (PRMC), which was headed by the Finance Minister. The Committee was tasked to examine and propose reforms to the powers, procedures, practices, organization and facilities of the National Assembly. An initial consultation, designing and planning period (Parliamentary Reform Project I, or PRPI) was followed by a round of reforms (under the Parliamentary Reform Project II, or PRPII) which took place from 2003 to 2007.

Parliamentary Reform Programme I – recommendations

Under PRP I, the PRMC was tasked with the study and drawing up of recommendations regarding reforms in the areas of: (i) the committee system, (ii) the legislative process, (iii) the administration of the National Assembly, (iv) support services to Parliament and its members, and (v) member–constituency relations.

The committee held discussions with parliamentary delegations from the Gambia, Germany, the Netherlands, the United Kingdom, the United States and Uganda, held meetings with other National Assembly committees, organized workshops and commissioned background papers. In its recommendations for reforms, amendments to the standing orders were proposed with the aim of, *inter alia*, improving the legislative process. The justification was that the National Assembly's ability to assert its autonomy and independence was severely impaired by the financial and logistical obstacles to introducing private-member legislation.

It was felt that, in order for the National Assembly to best represent the views of citizens in the policy-making process, the legislative process should be open, consultative and deliberative. None of these criteria existed at that time and it was thought desirable to develop a professional bill-drafting capability within Parliament that would allow members' proposals to be put into proper legislative language and form[1]. This was considered particularly important, as the intention was to have private members' bills become a key component of the National Assembly's legislative process. The committee therefore proposed that MPs should be allowed to submit bills during each session of the National Assembly at no cost to them as individuals. It was further recommended that the standing orders indicate a specific and appropriate time period between the publication of a bill in the gazette and first reading to allow for timely notification and public consultation and that each bill be accompanied by a fiscal impact statement detailing estimated costs and net benefits of the proposal.

Regarding member–constituency relations it was recommended that constituency offices be created, that parliamentary communications/outreach activities be enhanced and that the capacity for the delivery of constituent services be enhanced. It was felt that constituency offices, with appropriate staff, offer both MPs and constituents an official place to exchange ideas and information vital to carrying out the representative function of the elected member. Underlying this were the assumptions that a well-informed electorate is an important component of any healthy, stable democracy; that members who create close ties to the various groups, organizations, and individuals in their constituencies are most likely to thrive as a policymakers; that outreach efforts are an effective and important way of both disseminating and receiving information; and that effectively representing the interests and problems of constituents and constituency groups often requires the day-to-day efforts involved in assisting constituents. It was recommended that each MP should have an office located within his or her constituency and that costs would include renting of office space, equipment, phone lines, furniture, staff, training, and if necessary, security. MPs reacted favourably, and suggested that, while permanent offices were being established, they should be provided with resources to rent office accommodation. Funding of all recommendations pertaining to establishment of constituency offices was recommended to be part of the annual budget of the Parliament.

Other recommendations made during PRPI included that:

1 Literature should be made available to constituents, and include contact information for Parliament;
2 A directory of the National Assembly should be created, listing members of parliament, their photographs and contact details;
3 MPs should hold meetings for small gatherings of constituents on a regular basis at varying locations throughout the constituency;
4 Radio and/or television coverage for sessions of Parliament should be instituted;
5 MPs should utilize the news media as a vehicle for disseminating information on particular bills of policies.

Parliamentary Reform Programme II – implementation

Under PRP II, several amendments were made to the standing orders to improve the legislative processes, as well as with regard to oversight of the budget by the National Assembly.

In 2006, the standing orders were reviewed and amended, to bring them in line with current global trends in the practices and procedures of parliaments. The revised standing orders have since been published and contain a number of innovative features that promise to improve the quality of parliamentary processes. They include the use of a secret ballot in the election of the Speaker and Deputy Speaker; the establishment of question time for the vice-president every week; a reduction in required period of notice for private members' motions; and the requirement that Parliament meet the expenses related to the preparation of private bills. In addition:

1 Parliamentary sessions and committee meetings were opened to members of the public and media for the first time;
2 Live parliamentary debates were carried on television;
3 The work of Parliament's committee meetings was publicized through the parliamentary website and media more generally.

The PRMC also informed the National Assembly about the inputs to the Governance Sector Advisory Group's Fifth National Development Plan (FNDP), with the resulting inclusion of parliamentary reforms in the FNDP. These reforms focused on improving and developing member–constituent relations through improved communication, and development of an outreach program, as well as continued amendment or revision of the standing orders to further ensure effective legislation and the design and implementation of a legislative information system.

Constituency offices[2]

Under PRPII, eleven pilot constituency offices were launched, with the objective of increasing communications between constituents and members of parliament. Subsequently, 28 constituency offices were established, spread over 12 provinces; their selection was based on the following criteria:

1 Gender representation
2 Political party representation
3 Rural/urban mix
4 Geographic distribution across provinces
5 Constituencies whose member of parliament held ministerial portfolios and/or was a member of the Committee on Reforms and Modernization were eligible.

The earlier pilot and travel budget offices were all operating from rented accommodation, except for a few that were hosted in government buildings. Consequently, the total cost of rental for all offices was substantial. It was recommended that the National Assembly buy the buildings that would accommodate constituency offices.

In its 2006 report, the PRMC reported that the biggest challenge of the parliamentary reform programme was to sustain the operations of the existing constituency offices and continue to expand to other new constituencies. The constituency office project requires large sums of money to operate, mostly paid by donors. The executive, through the Ministry of Finance and National Planning, was advised by the committee to continue to fund constituency offices once donor support ended. Currently all 150 constituencies have these offices established and are operating in them. In all these constituencies the offices are in the form of a building that enables the local community in a constituency to see and meet their MP. The offices do not belong to the political party that the MP belongs to, or to any other political party, and are not used for partisan political activities. The goal is to allow constituents to have increased contact with government and increase the power sharing between parliament and the people.

It had been recommended by the PRMC that MPs be allowed to employ their own staff for the constituency offices. However, in line with keeping a professional and non-partisan cadre of constituency staff, the practice adopted was for the National Assembly to employ in consultation with the MP. Citizens can visit the offices in order to learn or get more informed on particular bills or debates.

With regard to other outreach activities, the outcome is mixed. MPs and their staff have not undertaken regular visits to schools and colleges in their constituencies – originally suggested so that they could introduce themselves and explain the overall workings of the National Assembly. However, more schools have visited Parliament.

Results

The PRMC reports a significant and positive change with respect to the constituency offices project, with a large number of people utilizing the facilities, an increased interface between MPs and their constituencies and improved quality of MPs' responses to people's concerns regarding developmental issues. The PRMC further reports that the monies received by constituency offices are also being spent well and accounted for.

Research by the Parliamentary Liaison Program undertaken by Caritas Zambia indicates that there is widespread support for constituency offices and the steps taken by government and supported by donors to 'decentralize' Parliament. The research confirms that constituency offices receive a good number of visitors and that in many instances such offices have been able to address the concerns of the people. Knowledge of Parliament is increasing. In one constituency, more than 300 visits were recorded in a single month, with most constituents being impressed with the positive response from the MP and his staff. At the same time, the MP stated that having a constituency office made it easier for him to respond to local needs and bring those needs before Parliament.

The PRMC also reported the need for strong political will on the executive side to reform and transform Zambia's parliamentary system, practices and rules. The National Assembly on its own cannot move very far without the requisite political support at the highest level. This is more so considering the fact that funding for the National Assembly comes from the national treasury. There is also need for the executive to be committed to seeing a parliament that is truly independent. The political will to change is also required to come from within Parliament itself.

Notes

1   The capacity to draft its own legislation in a competent and confidential manner without reliance on the executive strengthens the independence and power of a legislature.

2   Parliament is an integral part of governance because of its composition of leaders representing a cross section of society. However, the authenticity of the MPs has on many occasions been questioned by the electorate as they rarely integrate and share experiences of contact with government and experience of public service provision with their representatives. Many people in the constituency feel their wishes and aspirations are not adequately addressed, as they only get to see their members of parliament during campaigns. To address this state of affairs, the establishment of constituency offices – where an MP can carry out his/her work at the local level – are established to improve contact with the electorate and strengthen the relations between members of parliament and their constituents/constituencies.

7 Promoting reforms in the Kenyan Parliament
We have come a long way

Peter Oloo Aringo

I have recently met people who point out to me, excitedly, that the Kenya Parliament has made unimaginable changes in its operations, become more open and assertive; and obviously become the centre of national governance in the country. Newspaper editorials have recently made reference to the robust departmental and watchdog committee activities of the Kenya Parliament. The live broadcast of Parliament's proceedings is the most popular feature of media activity in Kenya. All these are hailed as historic achievements. However, very few people understand where all these began and the pain it took to get here.

To clearly understand these developments, one needs to cast an eye over the history of Kenya's Parliament. Largely inherited from the colonial government, the Kenya Parliament, known during the colonial period as the Legislative Council (LEGICO), was created purely to rubber-stamp the colonial government's decisions and give legitimacy to the colonial government's control of colonial Kenya's economy.

Unfortunately, the independence constitution neither paid attention to the institutional power of the legislative arm of government, nor made any effort to recreate parliament to reflect an independent country's representational imperatives. The independence constitution was a panel-beating job of the colonial constitution. Most of the features and vestiges of the colonial government's conceptualization of parliament's role in governance remained intact.

It is instructive to note, however, that Parliament had a real chance of growing to become a real representative body and a sensible decision-making and national leadership institution with the parliamentary system of government at independence. Jomo Kenyatta, Kenya's independence leader, was sworn in and received executive power as the prime minister, ruling the country from Parliament. This was modelled on the British system of government. It did not last long. When Kenya became a republic in 1964, one year into independence, and attempted to marry the British and American systems of government, thanks to the bipolar politics of the Cold War, Kenya's constitution became a mongrel mixture of presidential and parliamentary systems of government. As could be expected, one system was subordinated to the other. Clearly, in our case, the presidential system, in its crude and ambiguous form, became the overriding approach to government.

The resultant effect was a highly centralized system of government where the presidency was the centre of power, with unfettered and all-encompassing political power. The presidency was the alpha and omega of Kenya's national management. The president was everything. Parliament was a feeble rubber stamp of the executive branch's decisions. The independence Parliament was living in the unchanged tradition of the colonial Parliament which was in place mainly to ratify the decisions of the crown administration of Her Majesty the Queen. In the case of Kenya, Her Majesty the Queen was replaced at independence by the imperial president. The president ruled by decree, thinly veiled and dressed in the tunic of pretended parliamentary legitimacy.

The bipolar politics of the Cold War did not help matters. More concerned about checking the spread of communism, the West supported Kenya. No one objected as the Kenyan governance system moved more and more to a one-party dictatorship by the president with the rampant abuse of human rights, the controlled political space characterized by a muzzled press, detention without trial and a programme of reconditioning the constitution to specifically strengthen the presidential dictatorship. Of course the greatest causality of all this was Parliamentary independence. From muzzling Parliament, the Kenyatta administration moved to literally hand-picking the members of parliament (MPs). MPs critical of the President were detained without trial, hounded out of Parliament on flimsy legal grounds, or murdered.

This situation continued during the Moi administration where, after the coup attempt in 1982, President Moi, in panic and with a focus on consolidating his hold on power, brought about a constitutional amendment that made Kenya a *dejure* one-party state. With this, KANU became more powerful than Parliament and assisted the President in controlling the country. The party controlled the political oxygen in the country. MPs lost their seats when the party expelled them from its ranks, the party chose candidates through a boardroom preliminary and all parliamentary business was first approved by the party. Any MPs that opposed the party position in Parliament lost their seats.

In addition to extremely controlled political space, Parliament was just a rubber stamp of the executive branch. Nothing demonstrates this better than the fact that in its first four decades of existence, between independence in 1963 and the year 2000, the Kenya Parliament effected a total of nine constitutional amendments, all of them brought about by the executive branch and all of them targeted at consolidating presidential power over the other two arms of government,[1] the judiciary and the legislature.

The most common joke at this point in Kenya's Parliamentary history is that if one looked for the address of the Kenya Parliament in the phone book, it was listed under the office of the president.

Against the backdrop of such control, the MPs and Parliament were far from independent. The executive branch (read the president) had another way of controlling the MPs: through their remuneration. MPs were very poorly remunerated, did not have technical or even personal staff to work with them, and worst of all, did not have office space to operate from. Unless an MP was a cabinet minister or assistant minister, they operated literally from the streets. In the capital, Nairobi MPs just moved from their houses to Parliament. As a result of poor remuneration, the MPs could neither afford decent accommodation, nor have decent reliable means of transport. Constituency work was difficult.

To compound MPs' woes and control, the president's office perfected the art of patronage of Parliament by dishing out handouts to MPs. A chronic vulgarization of the traditional African spirit of helping the needy in the form of holding public collections towards social-welfare causes like hospital bills, burial expenses, and so on, in the form of *harambees*, worsened the MPs' economic lives. MPs were expected, from their meagre and paltry earnings, to preside over *harambees* – public collection activities towards social welfare and economic development causes – virtually every weekend. This was an incredible order to sustain. Every Friday morning, the 'good boys' from Parliament could receive something from the various patrons of the political system, all of them residing in the executive branch. This not only demeaned Parliament, but also grossly undermined the independence of the institution.

In the meantime, Parliamentary business was some sort of alleluia expedition. MPs had no research service, a pitiful library, no system of obtaining any information and no technical staff. The staff of

Parliament were all employees of the public service controlled by the Public Service Commission in the office of the president. They could be deployed and redeployed at the whims of the system. Some staffers woke up in the morning working in Parliament and were later in the day posted as public administrators elsewhere. Therefore in addition to political control, the executive branch had the monopoly of information and technical capacity. All MPs could do is just literally say Amen to all the proposals made by the executive branch.

There was virtually no committee activity. The party controlled all committee activity and ensured the most loyal of its members ended up in the watchdog committees that hardly had any sittings. Committee sittings could be counselled from State House and most committee reports did not even make it to the floor of the House for consideration by the plenary.

In 1992 when, under international and local pressure, especially occasioned by the end of the Cold War, Kenya reverted to multi-party politics, the long journey to changing Parliament and its relationship with the other arms of government began. Although nothing much had happened in terms of constitutional changes in 1992 besides the amendment of the section of political parties, the mood of the country was slowly moving towards political pluralism and a reawakening.

The first multi-party Parliament after the 1992 amendment would soon discover that it was difficult to operate effectively without an independent staff and budget. This led to efforts to establish the Parliamentary Service Commission (PSC) through an act of parliament. This was a gigantic task. The executive branch under President Moi was strongly opposed to this. The long journey to bring legislation to Parliament to establish such a commission started. Those of us who were committed to this started work with civil society organizations such as the Centre for Governance and Development (CGD) to draft the Parliamentary Service Commission Bill. Bilateral aid agencies like the United States Agency for International Development (USAID) and the British Department for International Development (DfID), working through Kenyan civil society organisations (CSOs), supported our efforts to draft the bill, edit it, publish it and get it to Parliament.

We went to the 1997 general elections before the bill could be taken through Parliament. By the time the eighth Parliament was sworn in, early 1998, many members were convinced of the need for autonomy and independence of Parliament that would only come through the establishment of an independent commission to handle Parliament's budget and institutional development.

After a tortuous road, the Constitution of Kenya (Amendment) Act establishing the PSC was enacted on 11 November 1999 and assented to by the President on 17 November 1999. It came into effect on 19 November 1999. This entrenched the Commission in the Constitution and was later followed by the introduction and enactment of the Parliamentary Service Act on 28 November 2000, during the eighth Parliament.

The Commission comprises ten members, of whom three are appointed and seven are elected. The Speaker of the Kenya National Assembly chairs the Commission and is assisted by a vice-chair who is elected by the other members of the Commission.

Apart from the vice president, who is also a member of the Commission, the rest of the Commissioners are members of the back bench elected from the various political parties. Four of these members are from the government side and three are from the opposition. The Clerk of the National Assembly is the secretary to the Commission.

The PSC oversees the institutional functions of Parliament by overseeing the Clerk and his staff, the recruitment and assignment of staff, staff development and the allocation of funds to the various committees. Since its establishment, a more autonomous and independent Parliament has had several milestones, including the development and launch of Parliament's first Strategic Plan for the years 2000–2012, the acquisition and refurbishment of Continental House to provide office space for members of parliament and the acquisition and refurbishment of County Hall to house the offices of the Parliamentary Service Commission, staff offices, some committee rooms and a large conference room.

Parliament, with its new-found autonomy, moved to improve MPs' constituency work by enacting the Local Government Transfer Act of 1998 to supplement the revenue of the local authorities nationwide to run and service certain local services. This was the forerunner to the popular Constituency Development Fund (CDF). This was followed by the Commission helping establish offices for MPs in both the constituencies and in the headquarters in Nairobi.

The Commission then moved to strengthen the secretariat of Parliament by establishing a recruitment, training and compensation scheme for staff of Parliament, now independently hired by the PSC. It also established technical directorates in Parliament in order to afford Parliament in-house expertise in legislative analysis and bills drafting, budget analysis and even policy analysis.

To afford members financial comfort and thereby independence from executive-branch patronage, the PSC guided MPs to pass the

National Assembly Remuneration (Amendment) Act, 2003. This gave members enhanced compensation for their services and allowed them to better concentrate on legislation.

The effect of these changes is so clear, including the increased volume of bills debated and passed by Parliament, especially during the ninth and now the tenth Parliament.

The quest for parliamentary autonomy and independence gained momentum, with new and better remuneration for MPs. The working conditions of parliamentarians have improved tremendously, with all the facilities brought about by the independent PSC. Thanks to these changes, Parliament has acquired technical expertise to address a number of critical institutional reforms in Kenya. Two of these have recently stood out clearly.

First, Parliament sought to participate more effectively in the national budget process. The executive branch has historically controlled all aspects of the budget process. However, parliamentarians with support from bilateral agencies and Kenyan CSOs commenced the initiative to give Parliament more leverage over the budget process. This saw the enactment of the Fiscal Management Act (FMA), which came into force on 19 June 2009. This law provides for the establishment of a Parliamentary Budget Office and Budget Committee through a statute, therefore giving them a legal status. The two had initially been established through a resolution of the House. This also means that Parliament is now actively involved in the budgetary process by reviewing and reporting on the annual estimates.

The new law gives Parliament a major role in budget oversight. It empowers Parliament to actively participate in the budget-making process by providing for direct consultations between portfolio committees and respective line ministries. The finance minister tables the budget policy statement (BPS) no later than 21 March each year. What the BPS is supposed to do is clearly provided in the law; to state the broad strategic macroeconomic issues that will be the basis of the budget of the succeeding financial year and the medium term. In doing so, Parliament has an opportunity to interrogate the rationale behind state allocations of resources long before the estimates are finalized.

Once the estimates of revenue and expenditure (budget) are laid in the House by the Minister, the FMA provides that they (the estimates) are sent to departmental/portfolio committees for scrutiny. These relevant committees scrutinize the estimates and meet the ministers and accounting officers in charge of relevant departments. Each committee is then to prepare a report before 21 days have elapsed since the estimates were first laid before the House.

The Act has also opened up the budget process to inputs by civil society and the private sector in a structured manner through the committee hearings. It also provides a framework for ensuring that spending agencies, ministries and departments account for previous budgetary allocations before new allocations are approved – the minister is to lay (together with the budget) a treasury report specifying, by department, all the measures taken by the government to implement the audit recommendations made by the National Assembly in the previous year.

One other important development as a result of the enactment of the FMA is that it provides a framework for Parliament to be informed of the policy intentions of the executive well in advance (i.e. through the budget policy statement in March each year). This strengthens Parliament's oversight role on the development and implementation of development policies by the executive.

A second and perhaps landmark reform introduced by Parliament, courtesy of the independence and autonomy acquired by the introduction of the PSC, is the review and institution of new House rules by the ninth Parliament. The Parliament revised the standing orders to make it more modern and responsive to the needs of an increasingly open environment.

The highlights of the changes brought about by the new standing orders include an expanded committee system. There are now a total of 28 committees, of which three focus on oversight committees, 13 on government departments and 8 are select committees. This increase in the number of committees emphasizes the role of committees in parliamentary practice.

The new standing orders have also seen enhanced regulation of committees. A stricter mechanism for ensuring discipline in committee work has been introduced. Among other provisions, there are general rules for public access to sittings, procedures for removal of the chair by a no-confidence vote, enhanced frequency of meetings, sanctions for non-attendance, mandatory reporting obligations providing for biannual progress reports, and provision for engagement of experts.

Political party recognition in the House including committees is now enshrined in the new rules to make parliamentary practice supportive of the necessary political party culture for the growth of democracy. The new standing orders contain more express recognition of political parties in the House. The House Business Committee is to reflect the 'relative majorities of the seats held by each of the parliamentary parties'. And while the party or governing coalition 'shall have majority', 30 per cent of the membership must not be ministers. In constituting other select committees, the House Business Committee is obliged to ensure that each committee reflects the relative majorities of the seats held by the parliamentary parties. There is also a unique recognition of a 'Back Benchers Caucus' to fill the position of an official opposition in the event that there is no party meeting the necessary threshold.

The most significant aspect of the new standing orders, especially as far as the legislature's role in the adjudication of national resources goes, is the entrenchment of a new role for Parliament in the budget process, in the rules. The procedures respecting budget scrutiny are nothing short of a landmark innovation in the way the Kenyan Parliament will work. The new provisions maintain the constitutional balance regarding budget proposals. The Constitution effectively reserves in the executive the power to originate the budget. The old standing orders made feeble provisions regarding scrutiny. Parliament had marginal approval powers to consider the national budget. These powers were easily circumvented by a government-controlled House Business Committee which determined the sequence of parliamentary consideration of the ministry votes and the guillotine procedure was potent at ensuring blanket approval of crucial votes. The new standing orders provide intrinsic scrutiny provisions both at the antecedent stage to the presentation of the formal budget and after presentation of the estimates. Institutional preparedness and technical expertise is required to ensure the committees use this innovation effectively.

In addition to opening up all committee proceedings to the public, the new rules also provide for live broadcasting of house proceedings and a procedure for public petitions. The regulation of public petitions is simplified. There is a more definite mechanism for presentation of petitions on the floor, making formal comments on petitions, tracking of petitions which are committed to the government departments, and mandatory obligation on ministers to respond.

All these changes have placed the Kenya Parliament in a new class of strong, emerging democratic legislatures.

Note

1   One of the most notorious constitutional amendments was introduced by the Attorney-General in 1985, ridiculously removing the security of tenure of the attorney-general himself, the chief justice and the judges of the High and Appeals Court. This bizarre amendment vested the powers of appointing and firing all these officers in the president!

8 Benin
Citizen participation in the national budget debate via the Budget Committee (a note)

Soule Adam

Following the end of single-party rule in 1990, Benin experienced rapid political and economic liberalization. Despite the lack of a strong democratic tradition, the country has been relatively successful in this transition. Of course, given the developmental constraints it faces, as well as the newness of its liberal democratic institutions, significant impediments to good governance persist. This is because the existence of competitive elections does not, in and of itself, guarantee an alignment of the interests between voters and civil society at large. Consequently, one mechanism by which a closer alignment of interests has been fostered, between public institutions and voters, is the participation of civil society in the scrutiny of the budget and other public-sector activities.

The National Assembly has played a significant role in this process, both by proactively trying to engage with members of civil society via its Budget Committee and by responding to and taking into account the recommendations of (some) civil society actors. Of course, given the resource constraints faced by civil society as well as the existence of rent-seeking interest groups and intransigent political actors, the magnitude of social accountability generated by such an exchange should not be overstated. Nevertheless, this process has resulted in tangible improvements in outcomes, even if it is no panacea. As this note, using the formal and informal interaction of civil society with the budgetary process of the National Assembly, aptly illustrates.

The role of the National Assembly in financial oversight: legal framework

The 1990 Constitution of Benin provides for a system of separation of powers in which the National Assembly, elected every four years, is a critical component. Specifically, Article 79 of the Constitution stipulates that:

> The Parliament shall be composed of a single Assembly called the National Assembly whose members (MPs) shall carry the title of Deputy. It shall exercise legislative power and shall control the action of the Government.

While Article 96 specifies that:

> The National Assembly shall pass the law and consent to the taxes.

Pursuant to its constitutional obligations, the National Assembly devotes its second session every year to the study and the passing of the Finance Act, which is submitted, to it, in draft form, by the executive (in accordance with Article 109 of the Constitution). However, despite the centrality of the budget, the Assembly faces significant problems in ensuring effective scrutiny of the said document. This is because of: (1) the complexity of the budget documents – prepared by technically oriented officials and thus not always comprehensible to many non-specialist MPs, and; (2) the limited technical assistance available to the Assembly, coupled with only 70 days in which to undertake scrutiny. Therefore, the challenge faced by the National Assembly has been how to effectively scrutinize the draft budget submitted to it before the vote (*ex-ante* scrutiny) as well as how to organize the effective monitoring of the budget's implementation (*ex-post* scrutiny).

One innovative way in which the Fourth National Assembly (elected in 2003) sought to achieve this objective was to launch an initiative involving citizens' participation in the review process. This is a significant departure from precedent as it is usual practice for the work of parliamentary committees to take place in private and not be accessible to the general public. This is despite the fact that the Internal Regulations of the House (Article 34 paragraph 7) states that:

> Committees may invite any person they deem it useful to consult, and, in particular experts and proponents of laws and resolutions. The experts may be heard at the request of the Parliament.

In order to satisfy this provision the Budget Committee of the National Assembly has opened its work to local expertise through the participation of professional associations, NGOs, civil society organisations (CSOs), trade unions, the National Association of Municipalities of Benin, the Association of Parents, the Chamber of Commerce, and others in the budget process.

In order to better understand the contribution of civil society to the National Assembly's work it is essential to outline the specific way in which the Budget Committee works and how it s role was enhanced by the activities of civil society.

1 – Organization of the work in a Budget Committee

(a) Structure of the Budget Committee

The Budget Committee is not explicitly mandated in the Constitution of Benin or the Internal Regulations of Parliament. Instead the following committees ordinarily merge for the purposes of undertaking these roles:

1   The Finance and Exchanges Committee (hereafter C2);
2   The Planning, Equipment and Production Committee (hereafter C3).

These two committees then form a joint committee known in Parliament as the Budget Committee which is co-chaired by the chairs of the C2 and C3. Formally the composition and role of the Budget Committee is:

1   MPs, members of the Budget Committee will share the responsibilities. Thus:

   •   The first rapporteur of C2 is designated as rapporteur for the budget
   •   The first rapporteur of C3 is the assistant rapporteur
   •   Each of the other MPs of the two committees is appointed as special rapporteur of the budget of a ministry or institution of the Republic. The role of the special rapporteur is to monitor and study the ministry's budget, to conduct any further investigations and report to the plenary of the budget committee. Specifically the Committee:

      •   Calls on the parliamentary administration to create an ad hoc secretariat for the timely preparation of the required volume of reports that MPs must be aware of before the passage of the draft budget.
      •   Stops the time schedule of budget work (including the appearance of ministers and institutions before the

Committee) and provides the government with a framework for implementation which must scrupulously be respected.

• Agrees on the list of CSOs which will be consulted on the budget and a copy of the entire budget project is mailed to each CSO involved in the discussions.

(b) Government information

Parliament communicates to the government the schedule of appearance of ministers and heads of institutions before the group that will hear the proposed budget of the said ministry or institution. The minister or the head of institution must present the budget himself and defend it by answering MP's questions.

2 – Capacity-building of MPs by the internal structures of Parliament

Two internal technical structures – the Unit of Analysis and Control of Budget Implementation (UNACEB) and the Policy Analysis Unit of the Parliament (CAPAN) – provide permanent support for Parliament. The UNACEB and CAPAN consist of top-level officers and university lecturers. The members of these committees are recruited on the basis of their skills and the independence they demonstrate in assisting MPs.

Furthermore, a training and information workshop for MPs is organized at which the draft budget is presented in a much more comprehensible manner. In particular the following topics are presented: the state of the economy, new measures/initiatives, anti-poverty programmes, the impact of the budget on gender issues and vulnerable persons. Finally, debates regarding new issues are encouraged in order to stimulate future policymaking. For instance, the 2009 workshop provided a forum for discussing the global economic crisis and its impact on Benin's economy.

3 – Participation of CSOs

Given that the state budget has an impact on social and economic development, it is normal for the National Assembly to hear the assessment of the budget by different groups of stakeholders. The procedure is as follows:

(a) At the opening of the session, the Budget Committee approves the list of partner CSOs

This list usually includes:

1 The Forum of National Organizations against Corruption (FNOAC)
2 Social Watch Network
3 Association for the Fight against Ethnocentrism and Regionalism (ALCRER)
4 The (central) Trade Union organization
5 The Federation of Associations of Parents and Students
6 The Chamber of Commerce and Industry of Benin
7 The Employers Association
8 The Association of Industries
9 The Association of Farmers
10 The National Association of Municipalities of Benin
11 The Association of Women Lawyers of Benin

Parliament provides a copy of the draft budget to each CSO, inviting it to analyze and evaluate the draft budget and to assess its impact on their respective field(s).

(b) Feedback on the analysis of CSOs to the Budget Committee

The CSOs are received one by one before the Budget Committee to present their analyses, their alternative proposals and, sometimes, their proposed amendments to the budget.

The beneficiaries and contributors to the budget participate actively in the debate. They express their concerns and priorities. They provide an avenue for MPs to decide on resource allocations to different sectors and later to monitor actual expenditures.

Relevant analyses are then made available to the Budget Committee; this process provides the MPs with more information with which to discuss and scrutinize the budget.

Thanks to these annual meetings a culture of communication is being developed between the National Assembly and citizens. By directly involving stakeholders in the debate on the general budget, the National Assembly has strengthened its legitimacy and effectiveness.

(c) Proactive work by civil society

Apart from the direct engagement of the Budget Committee with some members of civil society, other civil-society groups have also been working towards enhancing the social accountability of public institutions, thereby also providing the National Assembly with invaluable information and incentives to enhance its scrutiny powers. A good example of this is the work of Social Watch International. Via the establishment of workshops to aid understanding of the budget, the dissemination of information and research used to scrutinize and make budgetary recommendations, civil society was able to make significant contributions to the work of the National Assembly by identifying outstanding issues (for example problems in the budget allocation) and by proposing potential solutions.

Of course given resource constraints, mistrust by some elements of local government and bureaucratic intransigence the magnitude of these contributions needs to be kept in perspective. Still there is evidence that this exercise made a qualitative difference to good governance outcomes and to the National Assembly in exercising its scrutiny functions.

Conclusion

Despite enjoying a relatively successful transition to democracy, Benin's National Assembly faces significant challenges in fulfilling its role of ensuring scrutiny and oversight of the public finances. By formally engaging with members of civil society as well as assimilating information from other civil-society actors, the National Assembly has been able to increase its scrutiny function. Of course there is still room for improvement in this process, for more effective citizen participation in the debate on the budget. For example, CSOs could coordinate and consider the draft budget jointly in order to defend a common position before the MPs at committee hearings.

9 Strengthening financial accountability and parliamentary oversight in the Federal Republic of Ethiopia

Mesfin Mengistu

The public accounts committee (PAC) of the Federal Democratic Republic of Ethiopia was established in 2006 as part of an attempt to diffuse the political tensions that engulfed the country following the staging of the 2005 national elections. Specifically, the PAC was established in order to bolster the role of Parliament following allegations over post-election irregularities and an attempt by the outgoing Parliament to weaken the ability of opposition parties to participate in parliamentary procedures (the election results had just ensured that the new Parliament would include more opposition MPs than ever before[1]). Thus, while the election process itself was deemed to be the most competitive and fair to date, concerns and allegations over post-election voting irregularities and partisan tactics culminated in increased tensions and even violence. Specifically, the outbreak of violence was triggered when the outgoing Parliament, in which the ruling party had held 97 per cent of the seats, amended the provisions for agenda setting in the House (the lower chamber of Parliament) in a manner that was deemed to diminish the power of the opposition. Specifically, the outgoing Parliament's amendment replaced the previously flexible requirements for agenda setting in the House with a stringent set of criteria. Many pundits viewed this reform as a means by which the ruling party would effectively prevent the opposition from tabling their own agendas for discussion in the House. Consequently, the amendment generated severe and intense criticism both within Ethiopia and by expert foreign analysts.

The main opposition coalitions, the Coalition for Unity and Democracy (CUD) and the United Ethiopian Democratic Forces (UEDF), stated that they would only accept the election results if the amendment regarding agenda setting was immediately reversed. The ruling party's rejection of this demand had the effect of generating splits in opinion within the CUD and the UEDF. Some party members and supporters now advocated accepting the election results while other members continued to believe that pressing on with their demands was the best course of action. The majority of the CUD's leadership decided that the party's interests would be best served by following the latter strategy of non-acceptance of the status quo. Consequently, the party declared a 'public struggle' and sought to mobilize public opinion in its favour. This resulted in escalating tensions, with violence erupting between supporters of the ruling party and the opposition. This situation culminated in the loss of lives, massive detention of opposition supporters, and the destruction of property.

Despite the escalating violence, the ruling party steadfastly refused to reverse its position regarding the agenda-setting amendments to the Rules of the House, arguing that the reforms were essential to ensure the efficient functioning of Parliament. However, the ruling party did attempt to diffuse the situation and address concerns about parliamentary oversight by setting up and supporting a 'Democratic Gap Study'. The aim of this research project, which was carried out by a set of foreign experts, was to indentify a set of reforms that could enhance the role of Parliament by adopting the best practices of the parliaments in Canada, India, Germany and the United Kingdom. When the study group reported, one of its main recommendations was that the House of People's Representatives (HPR) should establish a PAC. Consequently, after a series of negotiations were conducted amongst the political parties of the House, the PAC was established.[2]

Membership and chairmanship of the committee

The organization and composition of the PAC is closely modelled on the modus operandi of the 'Department Related Committees' (DRCs) of the Indian Parliament. The main difference between the composition of the Ethiopian PAC and its Indian counterpart is that the former's membership is drawn from only the lower chamber of Parliament as opposed to the Indian case in which committee membership is drawn from both chambers.

Membership of the PAC is based on political party representation in the lower house and is, ordinarily, for the duration of the parliamentary term. The political party leadership within Parliament determines individual PAC membership, which is then formally ratified by the House. The total number of PAC members is 20. This is in line with all other committees of the House and is a requirement stipulated by Article 149 of the House's Code of Conduct. It is important to note that prior to the modification of the Code of Conduct the number of members on any committees had been 13. This modification of the Code of Conduct was also one of the ways in which the post-2005 election crisis had been diffused – it was designed to ensure that more opposition MPs could participate in the committee system.

Given these regulatory stipulations and the balance of power in the House, the following five parties are represented on the PAC:

1 The Ethiopian People's Revolutionary Democratic Front (EPRDF), 14 members
2 The Coalition for Unity and Democracy (CUD), 2 members
3 The United Ethiopian Democratic Forces (UEDF), 2 members
4 The Oromo Federal Democratic Movement (OFDM), 1 member
5 The Ethiopian Democratic Party (EDP), 1 member

Despite the diversity of party representation, the government enjoys an absolute majority of seats on the Committee. Unfortunately, the ruling party has used its majority position in a manner contrary to the spirit of consensual cooperation and independence that was supposed to characterize the working affairs of the PAC. This has, consequently, had the effect of complicating the Committee's ability to exercise effective and independent oversight of the executive.

However, despite the dominance of the governing party, the Chairperson of the PAC, me, is a member of the opposition. I am a member of the EDP, which was rewarded with the Chairmanship position due to the constructive role the party played in the negotiation process. The Deputy Chairperson and the members of the heads of the two subcommittees are from the governing party.

The functioning of the committee

The functions the PAC carries out are stipulated by: (1) the Code of Conduct of the House (Article 176) and; (2) the Rules of Procedures and Members' Code of Conduct of the House (Regulation No. 3/2006) and include the following activities:

1 Follow up and supervise the effective implementation of any budget allocated to the federal government by the House.
2 Scrutinize the report of the auditor-general. Specifically, the PAC is expected to pay close attention to and make sure that:

   a) any budgetary expansion was justified given the change in costs of the service it was supposed to finance;

b) any new expenditure undertaken was approved by a competent authority;

c) with respect to a transfer of budget, any such transfer was consistent with the relevant financial laws.

3   Evaluate the findings of the property auditing made by the auditor-general by order of the House.

4   Where expenditure by any government body: (1) exceeds what has been allocated to it within a fiscal year, and; (2) where the Committee finds it necessary to make an inquiry into the reasons that necessitated such excess expenditure; the PAC shall have the responsibility of submitting reports and recommendations to the House.

5   Supervise and follow up the effective implementation of the country's policies, laws, strategies, programmes and plans that relate to the functions of the committee.

Uncertainties that the new committee faced and questions it raised

Despite Ethiopia's relatively long parliamentary tradition, the idea of having a PAC had never been discussed or attempted prior to the establishment of the current Committee. Therefore, the newly established Committee had to start its work by developing a conceptual framework focusing on what its legitimate role should be. In order to facilitate this process a comparative fact-finding analysis was undertaken concerned with identifying the best practices of PACs in other countries. Of particular interest was how foreign PACs had been able to combine their universal functions of oversight to take into account the pre-existing traditions and sensibilities that govern the relationship between parliamentary committees and their respective referring House. More specifically the roles and functions of PACs in other countries were scrutinized to establish the extent to which PAC activities were commensurate with pre-existing expectations of executive oversight. This process, of comparative analysis, raised some interesting questions including:

1   How a PAC can effectively undertake the above listed functions?

2   What kind of relationship should be created and maintained with other standing committees?

3   Especially with respect to utilizing and scrutinizing the reports of the auditor-general?

The reason an extensive analysis of the relationship between the auditor-general and other standing committees was essential was due to the fact that it was realized, from an early stage, that there were no procedural mechanisms which could compel Parliament's departmental committees to follow a consistent approach in scrutinizing the auditor-general's reports. However, it was helpful to note that previous experience suggested that all oversight committees took close account of the findings of audit reports submitted to the House by the Office of the Federal Auditor-General (OFAG).

Is the committee really a PAC or another type of financial oversight committee?

Given the long history of the interaction between the auditor-general and departmental standing committee one of the major factors that needed to be considered and clarified at the onset was whether the auditor-general's audit reports should be scrutinized exclusively by the new PAC or whether other standing committees should continue to scrutinize these reports in any manner they deemed appropriate.

This concern, over the role of the PAC, given the pre-existing interaction between the auditor-general and departmental committees, came to the fore partly due to the ambiguity surrounding the name of the PAC. The official publication of the Code of Conduct of the House contains both the Amharic and the English translation of the Committee name. The English part of the Code explicitly refers to the new Committee as a public accounts committee. However, the Amharic part of the Code refers to the Committee using a name that potentially obfuscates its remit. Literally translating the Amharic version, the Committee's name is the 'Standing Committee on Government Expenditure and Management Control Affairs'. As, in virtually all the parliaments of democratic countries, the PAC is not the only committee engaged in the financial oversight of the executive, the Committee's Amharic name raised question regarding the exact role of the Committee and whether this would be consistent with the role that PACs play in other countries.

Does the committee's oversight only extend to the expenditure side and/or the revenue side of the government's accounts?

The Amharic name of the Committee suggests that the Committee would play a limited role with respect to oversight of government accounts. This limited role contrasts with the historic establishment of the British PAC, which emerged as a product of parliamentary debates regarding public expenditure. The British PAC was established in 1860 to 'examine the accounts showing the appropriation of sums granted by the parliament to meet the public expenditure of and such other accounts laid down before parliament as the committee may think fit'. Thus, the British PAC was given the right to examine both expenditures (explicitly) and revenues (tacitly). The Indian PAC, which follows the conventions of its British counterpart, regularly examines the revenue receipts of the government of India.

However, despite the Amharic name of the Committee, there is no provision in the Rules of the House, which stipulates that the PAC should only examine revenues and not expenditures. Furthermore, the auditor-general's reports to the House include an analysis of both the expenditure and the revenue side of the government's accounts and our Committee is clearly mandated to investigate such reports. Therefore, the problem of ambiguity is generated by the name rather than the actual rules that govern its work. Given these contradictory factors, we felt it was better to clarify the issue immediately and raised the question of whether the new Committee's remit was only to focus on the oversight of expenditure management or not.

Does the Ethiopian PAC have the power to evaluate policies?

Following international best practice, the PAC is concerned with issues of economy, efficiency and the implementation of government policy. As one of the reports on the Canadian PAC noted '...the Public Accounts Committee (PAC) is not fundamentally concerned with matters of policy. The Committee does not call in to question the rationale of government programs, but rather the economy and efficiency of their administration.' McGee confirms this principle by stating that 'PACs concentrate on how policy is implemented, rather than on the policy itself.'[3]

What is the relationship between the PAC and the auditor-general?

In the consultation meetings we conducted with the group of expatriate experts we were told that the PAC's work is largely dependent on the findings of the reports of the auditor-general. Consequently, we tried to frame our work based on this insight. However, how the relationship between the Committee and the auditor-general will evolve in practice is not clear and is confounded by the legal context that governs our interaction, which leaves many questions unanswered. For example:

1   Sub-article 3 of Article 176 states that the Committee 'shall evaluate the finding of property auditing made by the Auditor-General on the order of the House.' However, this clause does not address whether the Committee has the right to scrutinize the findings of property auditing made by the auditor-general without the order of the House?

2   Sub-Article 4, '...[w]here expenditure by any government body exceeds what has been allocated within a fiscal year, and where the Committee finds such additional expenditure in excess, it shall have the responsibility of submitting reports and recommendations to the House.' As stated, this function of the Committee suggests that it has competencies beyond investigating the reports of the auditor-general. But it is unclear whether this means that this particular responsibility can be performed without using the auditor-general as a channel of information.

The present working procedure of the committee

The Committee has been working within the general framework stipulated by the Code of Conduct of the House with respect to the operation of all standing committees. The Code of Conduct, in addition to constituting the specific undertakings of each standing committee, also establishes modalities for the general operation of committees. All standing committees in the House are mandated 'to follow up and supervise government bodies, to initiate laws, to examine witnesses and documents, to undertake studies relating to the objectives for which they are organized to perform and other duties assigned by the speaker.'

The Code of Conduct also establishes conventions regarding how each standing committee should work. Each standing committee is expected to supervise and follow up on the work of government bodies (Article 155). Furthermore, this article stipulates that committees are mandated to prepare their own reports to the House, which should include recommendations regarding any problems they encountered in the process of supervising and following up the work of relevant government bodies.

Given the newness of the PAC, considerable debate emerged regarding its proper role and functions. The membership of the Committee decided that the best modus operandi should be to emphasize the need for consensus building and a focus on technical assessment rather than a controversial and possibly partisan political focus. This approach required us to develop a clear understanding regarding the specific tasks and the nature of oversight that the PAC was expected to undertake.

Finally, given the rules stated in the Code of Conduct, it was agreed that the Committee should base all of its work on the reports of the OFAG.

The relationship between the PAC and the auditor-general

As noted above, our survey of the working practices of other PACs revealed that a good relationship between the PAC and the auditor-general is critical if the Committee is to achieve its objectives of financial oversight. As McGee notes '...historically PACs were created to ensure parliamentary follow-up on Auditor-General's report, and because the jurisdiction of PACs has more in common with Auditor-General's remits than does that of other committees.'[4] However, in practice, this working relationship varies, from country to country, based on a number of country-specific attributes.

In Ethiopia, the auditor-general is a constitutionally mandated legislative officer. In other words his office, the OFAG, is a parliamentary institution. Furthermore, the functions of the OFAG are stipulated in the constitution, which states that OFAG '...shall audit and inspect the accounts of ministers and other agencies of the Federal Government to ensure that expenditures are properly made for activities carried out during the fiscal year and in accordance with the approval allocations, and submit his reports thereon to the House of Peoples' Representatives.' Furthermore the constitution stipulates that OFAG should directly submit its annual budget to the House for approval. In the House, the PAC is mandated to oversee the compatibility of the auditor-general's operation alongside its function of investigating the reports that the auditor-general produces after auditing government departments. Therefore, the PAC receives two kinds of reports from the auditor-general, performance reports of his office and the multitudes of other audit reports.

In examining the performance report submitted, the PAC's aim is to: firstly, approve the auditor-general's annual plan at the beginning of the year; secondly, based on this approved plan and a quarterly report on progress, the Committee scrutinizes the performance of the auditor-general's progress at quarterly intervals. The examination process involves measuring the performance, analyzing any failings and asking for clarifications over issues raised in these reports. The PAC also conducts public hearings and sends feedbacks and recommendations to the auditor-general himself as well as the Speaker of the House.

The establishment proclamation of the OFAG also empowers the auditor-general to present a summary of his performance report once a year directly to the House in plenary session. The PAC, as the relevant oversight committee of the auditor-general, is mandated to facilitate this annual report according to the stipulations of the Code of Conduct of the House.

In the process of investigating the audit reports, the PAC also frequently summons the auditors who produced the report under investigation for further elaboration and/or these auditors are requested to attend hearings as PAC witnesses.

Meetings of the Committee

The regularity and nature of PAC meetings are stipulated in the Code of Conduct of the House. Specifically, Article 136 of the Code of Conduct details all necessary procedures required for a committee meeting while Article 152 stipulates the specific procedures of such meetings. The articles stipulate that every standing committee should sit twice a week, on Monday and Wednesday from 9.00am–12.30pm and from 2.30pm–5.30pm. Attendance is compulsory for all committee members.

The Code also stipulates that, if the chairperson of a committee considers it necessary, a committee can conduct additional meetings (irregular meetings). If an agenda needs to be discussed jointly by two or more committees, the committees in question can organize a joint meeting under the leadership of the chairman of the committee whose remit of oversight is closer to the issue at hand. Furthermore, committee meetings are open to all MPs – as Sub-section 3 of Article 136 stipulates '[i]n the absence of any mandatory conditions to the contrary, members of the House who are not members of the standing committees may attend any sitting of Standing Committees without having the right to vote.'

The quorum requirement for a standing committee is an absolute majority (50 per cent +1) as stipulated in Sub-section 1 of Article 136. It is the responsibility of chairpersons to develop the agenda for the meeting and ensure that any preparations required for the meetings are realized e.g. by ensuring that documents for debate are available to all members beforehand. Committee meetings, including meetings of the oversight committees, are not held in public.

Given this regulatory framework, the PAC has been conducting its meetings in accordance with these existing guidelines and norms that govern the meetings of the House. However, meetings of any subcommittees are under the jurisdiction of the Committee. Consequently, PAC subcommittees usually conduct their own meetings as conditions require without being confined by any specific rule. Subcommittees are not formal forums of debating over issues under scrutiny, but rather are mandated only to work on technical issues, directed to facilitate regular meetings of the Committee, at the order of the Committee or its Chairperson.

The relationship with other committees

One of the most controversial issues regarding the establishment of the PAC is its relationship with other standing committees. Despite a series of prolonged discussions aimed at reaching a consensus on an agreed-upon working system for the Committee, including how it could cooperate with other committees, little was achieved in practice. This lack of clarity was confounded by the broad scrutiny functions of departmental oversight committees which, ordinarily, enjoy scrutiny over a department's: (1) yearly budget allocation; (2) administration of government property. Given the existence of such pre-existing scrutiny mechanisms it was difficult to determine how a new committee devoted to fiscal oversight could work in tandem within this framework and without generating conflict. Thus, while the PAC's work investigating the reports of the OFAG's performance reports has introduced new oversight mechanisms, the activities of the Committee with regards to departmental performance reports was considered an unnecessary interference and duplication of work undertaken by other committees.

After a series of debates, it was decided that the hearings that the PAC conducts, based on the findings of the auditor-general, should be undertaken in coordination with the standing committee responsible for the oversight of the relevant department. Consequently, the PAC has been conducting public hearings in coordination with each of the other standing committees. However, it is important to note that we on the Committee are disappointed with this decision, which we argue goes against identified international best practices of the PAC and erodes the Committee's independence.

Conclusion

The Public Accounts Committee of Ethiopia is a new committee whose establishment was due to political events rather than the result of a long and pre-existing desire to strengthen the accountability mechanisms of the Ethiopian Parliament. Following the traditions and practices of 'Westminster System Parliaments' the chair of the PAC is an opposition MP and the majority of PAC members are from the ruling party. The Committee is, therefore, dominated by a partisan bloc in a manner contrary to practices in some other countries. Furthermore, the PAC has been working in a very polarized political atmosphere and, despite efforts to create agreeable working procedure for the Committee, these have had limited success. I believe the next step in improving the effectiveness of the PAC should be to focus on ensuring enhanced effectiveness by establishing an acceptable working system of cooperation between the PAC and other committees, and consequently enhancing the PAC's capacity to undertake effective scrutiny.

Notes

1   The opposition parties/coalitions increased the number of seats they held from 11 out of 547 before the 2005 election to 170 out of 547 after the election.
2   Another critical reform that was enacted was the changing of the Code of Conduct of the House, which was reformed to incorporate many new other elements suggested by the study team.
3   David G. McGee, The Overseers: Public Accounts Committees and Public Spending, Commonwealth Parliamentary Association in Association with Pluto Press, London 2002.
4   Op. cit.

10 Rebuilding parliament in a conflict-affected country

Based on an interview with Senator Franklin Siakor from Liberia

Introduction

In the interview, Senator Franklin Siakor outlined his personal story and talked about the consequences of Liberia as a failed state and his realization, as a first-term senator, that corruption was pervasive and that a 'bottoms-up' approach to fighting corruption is required.

Participatory governance and representation

Senator Siakor believes that he can play a personal role in fighting corruption by encouraging participatory democracy via county level stakeholder meetings, community radio, women's group organizations and development and governance meetings at district level.

Despite the fact that he has had difficulty in ensuring meetings take place due to financial, time and travel constraints, he tries to travel around his constituency in order to ascertain the quality of public services.

He has attempted to introduce pro-poor budgeting into the national budget and uses constituency meetings to ascertain the needs of his constituents. A 'county development committee' has been set up to supervise and monitor the application of the Mittal Steel funds and the county development funds.

Budgetary limitations

Senator Siakor went around his county after the national budget to explain to constituents why the budget could not meet all their needs but how constituents might be able to take grass-roots action (service provision) to fill the gaps.

He facilitated a three-day county development meeting in partnership with the Development Education Network-Liberia (DEN-L) and the Bong County Reconciliation Committee chairperson, with funding from Search for Common Ground (SFCG) in order to establish budget priorities.

Self-help development projects

Senator Siakor and his staff have used county meetings to help actors achieve developmental goals via grass-roots action. For example: they have provided training and equipment for three community radio stations for which he purchased FM transmitters in 2006 and 2007. The training focused on the concept of community radio, newsgathering and reporting, interviewing techniques, programme production and broadcasting.

Struggles

Senator Siakor noted the collective action problems inherent in trying to ensure the provision of community services via volunteers.

Conclusion

> Collaboration is key in reaching what I want. I cannot do it alone, so I need to work with allies and compromise. That's not always easy. Legislators in the country are under pressure to donate to self-help projects since government budget is too limited to take care of most of the urgent local development needs.
>
> Senator Franklin Siakor

11 Changing the standing orders of Parliament in Tanzania

Willibrod Slaa

Introduction

The reform of parliament that took place in Tanzania can be classified as procedural, and relates to the rules that govern the way things are done within Parliament (the Bunge). Parliamentary standing orders regulate how Members of Parliament (MPs) perform their monitoring and legislative functions, and standardize internal rules and parliamentary procedures. Parliaments have attempted to alter their internal structures and working methods by reforming their rules of procedure or standing orders. Tanzania recently reformed its standing orders in an attempt to give Parliament more say in the way it carries out its business. Through the review of the parliamentary standing orders, the Bunge has introduced significant changes which can redefine its relationship with the executive and with the public in general.

Bunge

The Parliament of the United Republic of Tanzania, or Bunge as it is popularly known, has been grappling with an identity crisis since the country attained independence in 1961. The legislature has always found itself in the shadow of the National Executive Committee of the ruling party Chama cha Mapinduzi (CCM).

The political transition to pluralism in 1992 resulted in minimal institutional changes, and did not lead to great changes in the functions or identity of the parliament. The political culture in Tanzania remained unchanged, and the multi-party area brought few opportunities to influence decision-making at the legislative and executive level. Even though the national law was altered in 1992 to allow multi-party rule, the country had to wait until the parliamentary elections of 1995 to see any opposition parties elected to parliament for the first time. So for those two or three years, the Bunge had de facto only one party and parliamentary business continued as usual.

The legislature, dominated by CCM, continued to be used as an instrument to legitimize the party's decisions. Occasionally there were vigorous debates in the plenary, but the legislature had little autonomy in practice. The opposition had about 15 per cent of the total seats in the Bunge, and even today about 80 per cent of seats in Parliament belong to CCM members.

The legislature also suffered from the lack of a legal framework, and a lack of human and resource capacity to allow for real political participation. The Bunge did not benefit from any meaningful reforms and until 2008 it continued to be governed by the same parliamentary standing orders that existed during the one-party era.

Leading to a change in standing orders

After the elections in 2005 the review process of the rules of procedure of Parliament started. Reform of Parliament was needed, it was time for change. You could really sense a new mood in Parliament, and an appetite to get things done in a different way. There were constitutional and statutory limitations for the functioning of Parliament, as the standing orders still reflected much of the rubber-stamp parliament under one-party rule. The standing orders at that time dated from 1995, and, consistent with the parliament in the one-party era, did not give the Bunge sufficient tools to carry out its oversight, legislative and representation function properly.

I was part of a small group of bipartisan reformist MPs that came together because the Bunge was ready for change. A special committee was established to change the standing orders and consisted of seven people: two from the opposition and five from the CCM. Party issues were not relevant in the small committee because we all had one mind: we wanted to give Bunge teeth in order to improve its performance.

We felt that the ideas we were to propose had to be based on best practices and experiences of other countries. In order to gain this experience we travelled to India, Kenya, Mauritius, Zambia, Zimbabwe and Uganda, to look at good practices, other examples, commonalities, and to find ways to introduce and translate some of these ideas to Tanzania. Parliament provided the money that was necessary to travel, conduct research and to produce reports with recommendations on the standing orders. The recommendations from the special committee were very clear and obvious; they were difficult to critique and hard to go about. The special committee reported its findings to the Speaker, and the Speaker reported back to the full House. The recommendations were taken over by the Speaker, who was genuinely committed to the independence of Parliament. For one, he supported a clause in the new standing orders that pronounce clearly the impartiality of the Speaker in all matters in the House.

The government reacted by forming its own committee, which also visited the countries we visited. I think in the end this might have helped the CCM to better understand the need for changes in parliamentary procedures. Not only were members of the opposition ready for change, but several CCM members were also supportive of the proposed standing orders. However, it was not easy persuading the executive to adopt our recommendations. In 2007, together with the government, we went through each proposed amendment, rule by rule. It was a very difficult process: the proposed changes in standing orders were heavily resisted by some in the ruling party, and the government was not cooperative at all. Some of the original changes suggested by the select committee were quite radical. We negotiated with the executive, and the current standing orders are a compromise of that process. For example, at first the ruling party refused to adopt a question period for the Prime Minister, and made all efforts to block this suggestion. In the end, we came to a compromise and agreed that only current issues are allowed to be discussed during the question period.

The new standing orders

The new standing orders came into effect in January 2008. Because of these new parliamentary procedures, the Bunge can constructively and meaningfully participate in the decision-making process. Some of the major changes are:

1   Until 2008 the Bunge did not have any decision-making power in passing proposed bills or in approving the Budget. Parliament was not even allowed to make minor changes to a bill. It had no say in determining the country's budget priorities, or setting budget ceilings. The president was the one who made the final decision on any bill or the budget. On top of that, the president could dissolve the Bunge at any time. Under the new standing orders,

Parliament has a session, called the planning session or pre-budget session, that takes place each February and is reserved only for determining spending plans. Members can review government priorities before the individual committees sit in May to assess the estimates of various ministries. This is aimed at involving Parliament in the planning stages of the national budget, rather than only reviewing government expenditure, as it did previously. Through this session, the Bunge is now able to influence national policies, priorities and the budget of Tanzania;

2   An office of Legal Advisor to Parliament has been established to assist members in legislative drafting;

3   The rules governing the introduction of bills in the Bunge have also undergone some transformation. Before, only the government could propose bills. Under the revised standing orders, MPs can now introduce legislation through private members' bills, and standing committees are allowed to propose bills as well;

4   When government bills, private members' bills or committee bills are introduced, it is required to better inform the House and the general public about their intended effects. Therefore, they have to be accompanied by more comprehensive explanatory documents, and additional time between readings is required. The increased length of time will also be used to give the public time to comment on the bills before they are passed into law. Reforms in Parliament's budgetary process might increase the institution's efficiency, especially relating to the time it takes to scrutinize government spending. The budget process used to be very rushed but the new standing orders will provide for more time to allow MPs to deliberate on government estimates and expenditures. Instead of the usual 35 days, Parliament will now have 50 days to focus on the national budget;

5   The government is now required by law to respond to committee reports. For instance, discussion of the report of the Public Accounts Committee (PAC) was previously not required. The report was tabled in Parliament and maybe an MP would take on the initiative to raise certain issues, although in practice that almost never happened. The new rules require the report of the PAC to be discussed by Parliament. The PAC reports to Parliament with an analysis of the report of the controller and auditor general, and this triggers a two-day debate;

6   For the first time in the history of the Tanzanian Parliament, the prime minister must appear regularly in Bunge for 'prime minister's questions';

7 Because of the new procedures, it is now harder for MPs to malign or defame members of the public if they are not in a position to defend themselves on the floor of the House. An offended party may write to the Speaker within 14 days to complain against an MP who attacks their integrity while debating in the House. The Speaker will then submit the complaint letter to the disciplinary committee which investigates the matter and takes remedial action;

8 Individual MPs are now protected from being silenced or interrupted in the House. For instance, MPs or the Speaker can only interrupt a speaking MP if they can prove that what the speaking MP is saying is incorrect, thereby using clear evidence. This measure is especially beneficial to the opposition, who now have the opportunity to speak more freely. In practice, this has influenced the way MPs speak in the House as debates are much more open and vocal;

9 The new standing orders give more voice to the opposition by allocating the chairmanship of three of the four watchdog committees to a member of the opposition. The Public Accounts Committee, the Local Government Accounts Committee and the Parastatal Accounts Committee are now all chaired by members from the opposition. This also means that three opposition members will now sit in the Central Committee, which is the steering committee of Parliament, thereby boosting the opposition's voice in setting Parliament's agenda. The fourth watchdog committee, the Finance and Economic Committee, is chaired by the CCM;

10 Committees are now more transparent as the new standing orders allow them to open up to the press. For example, the watchdog committees responsible for overseeing government expenditures used to conduct their meetings in camera, behind closed doors. Opening up to the public and the press has definitely changed the course of events. The issues discussed at the committee level are highly sensitive. All this information is now immediately released into the public domain;

11 The new standing orders have given more power to the parliamentary committees. Committees are now not only empowered to order a person to appear in court by the issuance of a summons, they can also order special audits to be executed by the auditor-general and the comptroller if they feel an issue deserves to be looked into in more depth. The audit has to be reported back to Parliament, after which the government has to respond and take action.

Implications at the committee level

The new rules emphasize the traditional oversight role of parliamentary committees and make it easier for the Bunge to act out its oversight function effectively. The standing orders have been revised to enable more parliamentary debate as well. The right of MPs to speak freely within the National Assembly and to introduce legislation has resulted in more parliamentary investigations and better parliamentary oversight. The internal reforms have already produced some notable results, especially at the committee level. Strong committees are a minimal condition for effective parliamentary influence in the policy-making process. In Tanzania, committees are supposed to assist Parliament in exercising its surveillance powers over activities of the executive more effectively and efficiently. Two of the most apparent cases where the change in standing orders have made a difference and where Parliament has taken advantage of its increase in power are outlined below.

Newly created standing committees: the Parastatals Accounts Committee

Presently, there are 15 standing committees of the House, which is almost double the number (8) that existed during the one-party era. The increased number and permanence of these committees generates more favourable conditions for Parliament to act independently in the policy process, and provides the opportunity to build consensus between members of the executive and of the opposition parties. The standing committees are broadly divided into two categories: portfolio committees (exercising direct oversight over ministries or acting as 'shadow' ministries) and non-portfolio committees, of which there are five. Two of them, namely the Public Accounts Committee (PAC) and the Local Authorities Accounts Committee (LAAC) scrutinize the report of the controller and auditor-general to ascertain whether the monies appropriated by Parliament are spent as intended.

The most recent addition to the non-portfolio committees is the Parastatals Accounts Committee (PARAC), which commenced its work in 2008. The PARAC would not exist if it wasn't for the new standing orders. It was reintroduced after being abolished in 1995 because Parliament discovered the government has significant investments in parastatal organizations (such as electricity companies and the central bank). In fact, about 25 per cent of the Tanzanian GDP is invested in parastatals, meaning that a quarter of the national income was not subject to any form of oversight. The starting up of the Committee in

2008 was first proposed by the auditor-general and controller, after which the select committee looking into changing the standing orders took over the recommendation.

PARAC is chaired by a member of the opposition, while the rest of the Committee consists of CCM members. However, all committee members are like-minded and have managed to leave party issues outside the Committee. The Committee oversees 193 parastatal companies, and oversees privatization processes and companies in which the government has a share. Some parastatals are (partially) owned by MPs from the ruling party, resulting in a lot of criticism and resistance to PARAC's work. The Committee released its first report in April 2009. The government, now required to respond, answered on time with their own report. The experience has been very positive. As a result of PARAC's reports and the follow-up debates in Parliament:

1   the government introduced a department mandated to oversee parastatals from the government side;
2   parastatals have cut their costs and therefore increased revenues because they know they are now subject to committee oversight;
3   many parastatals have established an internal audit committee;
4   pension funds have reduced their reckless and risky investments significantly;
5   the government has returned investments it had taken from the mining company STAMICO so that the company is able to make its own investments again.

Newly created select committees

Under the new standing orders, Parliament is allowed to create select committees for the first time, at the discretion of the Speaker. Select committees can serve as support to the existing standing committees by looking into a specific matter in detail. The new standing orders made it possible to appoint a select committee to investigate a public controversy. This would have been very difficult under the old standing orders. According to the standing orders, MPs must notify the Speaker that they wish to appoint a select committee. They put their request in writing and then it will be put to a vote. All our committees are bipartisan. In the past, if such a request appeared inconvenient to government, a three-line whip would be imposed and the investigation would not happen. For example, in 2006 there was no request for any kind of investigation by Parliament.

Select committee investigating the Richmond Development Corporation

In 2007, following concerns raised by the Standing Committee on Trade and Investments, Parliament voted to establish a select committee to investigate an electrical power contract with Richmond Development Company. The Chairman of the Trade and Investment Committee insisted there was something that could not be explained about Richmond. All the members of his Committee agreed to recommend a select committee enquiry. By November 2007, Tanzania's first select committee was appointed, mandated to carry out investigations regarding a controversial electricity supply contract. The Committee's investigations found corruption at the core of an emergency power project meant to resolve the country's power crisis. The project had been awarded to US-based Richmond Development Corporation, later found to be unqualified and financially unviable. The Committee's report also implicated the Office of the Prime Minster, which influenced the extension of Richmond's contract by US$ 172.5 million to provide 100 megawatts of electric power, even after this service was no longer required. Several cases of lack of transparency were exposed, and the government was forced to correct them. In February 2008, then Prime Minister Edward Lowassa resigned after the committee presented a report of its investigation to Parliament, calling for the resignation of all top government officials implicated in the scandal. The conclusions of the enquiry also led to the resignation of two ministers, the Minister for Energy and Minerals (Nazir Karamagi) and the Minister for East African Cooperation (Ibrahim Msabaha). Dr. Edward Hosea, the Director General of the Prevention and Combating of Corruption Bureau, resigned as well. With the prime minister's position vacant, President Kikwete had no choice but to dissolve the cabinet.

Select committee investigating the Bank of Tanzania

In an equally riveting saga, a parliamentary committee was established to examine allegations of corruption surrounding the Bank of Tanzania (BoT). The first evidence of irregularities was uncovered during a routine audit by Deloitte & Touche. Monies from the external arrears account were alleged to have funded the CCM's 2005 election campaign. I had raised the BoT issue in Parliament for the first time in 2007, under the old standing orders. Unfortunately, but expectedly (at that time), I was shut down by the whip, CCM members and the Prime Minister. There was an immense influence that the Prime Minister had on CCM members who refrained from bringing up the issue for discussion in the Assembly. Despite several threats and other inconveniences, I just kept insisting to speak and discuss the matter, and I submitted a private member's motion. The Speaker prevented the alleged scam at the BoT from being tabled but because opposition members kept trying to raise the issue in Parliament, the story made headlines in the independent newspapers. Shortly after the change in standing orders a select committee was set up following pressure on the government by several MPs.

In August 2007 the CCM MP Mr Zitto tried to get the government to set up a select committee to investigate the controversial signing of the Buzwagi gold mining contract that took place in London, accusing the Energy and Minerals Minister of withholding the truth about this matter. The Speaker of the Assembly claimed that Mr. Zitto had been disrespectful to the minister and suspended him for four months under the provisions of the Parliamentary Immunities, Powers and Privileges Act (No.3 of 1988) which grants Parliament the authority to punish its own Members. When Mr. Zitto was suspended the opposition parties joined hands and together travelled to 12 regions in Tanzania to explain to the electorate what had happened both with the BoT and with the mining issue.

When we all came back to Parliament the new standing orders went into effect and we formed a coalition to raise both issues again in Parliament. You have to understand that there was now also pressure from outside, an outcry from our people to stop corruption. The standing orders were revised to enable more parliamentary debate and MPs now had the right to speak freely within the National Assembly. When the committee's report on BoT was tabled in Parliament MPs were able to discuss and debate the sensitive issues because of the new standing orders. This has benefited the BoT case because instead of silencing allegations, everything could be discussed openly.

The issue involves allegations of massive misappropriation of funds (exceeding $200 million) at the Bank of Tanzania. Dubious payments were made through the BoT's external commercial debt account. The Committee's report reveals that the Bank of Tanzania authorized fraudulent payments worth TSh133bn (US$ 120 million) as recently as 2005. Monies siphoned from the central bank had been disguised as overdue foreign-currency obligations under its external arrears account, a mechanism for regulating foreign-exchange transactions under the strict currency controls of the 1980s. The shortfall was underwritten by a government bond, issued by the outgoing administration of former President Benjamin Mkapa. Auditors found that local businessmen had colluded with bank officials to procure loans for at least 22 local companies.

The response to the scandal is among the most telling indicators of change in Tanzania's political body. In January 2008 the Central Bank governor resigned. A presidential commission, comprising the Attorney-General and Inspector General of Police, set a deadline for stolen funds to be repaid by 31 October 2008. About TSh50bn in cash had been recovered before the deadline. Some of the rest is understood to have been invested by beneficiaries in luxury properties in Dubai. In November 2008, the first legal charges arising from the Bank of Tanzania scandal were announced by state prosecutors. Although those who returned funds may hope to avoid prosecution, prominent parliamentarians have insisted that any amnesty must come from Parliament. The case shows how parliamentary committees are now exercising their power to subpoena public officials. This power existed before but it was never utilized. It is because of the gain in confidence and power that Parliament is not afraid to act on its rights any longer.

Parliament pressed for detailed investigations on other major contracts the government had signed with foreign investors. Initially the executive responded to Parliament's push for investigations on corruption by trying to silence the critics, especially those of the opposition. Numerous times I have stood up in Parliament when the government threatened to arrest MPs for having (secret) sensitive government documents. The report we produced in my Committee (the Local Accounts Committee) mentions the exact names of corrupt MPs and government officials, so I felt like the government was talking to me. I told them to come and arrest me because I have those sensitive government documents. Nothing ever happened; it turned out to be just threats. After the government's attempt failed, it was forced to take action, either by punishing those accused of misdeeds or by setting up select commissions to investigate matters further.

Future

Despite the recent review of its parliamentary standing orders, a move that aimed to give the Bunge more leeway in conducting its affairs, the reforms do not go far enough to grant real parliamentary independence from the executive. Parliament still lacks an important role in the budget process and administrative and financial problems still beset its effective functioning. The ruling party still dominates Parliament, both because of its simple majority and by its influence on most of its MPs. Committees have limited resources available to perform their oversight work effectively. The National Assembly does not have control of its own budget and instead receives money from a consolidated fund through the Treasury. Funding shortages sometimes make it difficult for committees to carry their oversight functions further, for instance by making site visits to investigate malpractice or monitor whether legislation is being implemented. Under the new parliamentary rules, committees are allowed to travel around the country to conduct investigations, but the standing orders do not allow Parliament to cover the costs for this type of visits. Therefore the World Bank sponsors all our watchdog committees to be able to conduct their oversight function effectively and pays for the committees' field visits.

The cases outlined above clearly show how the Tanzanian Parliament is changing. We are becoming much more effective because we are much more empowered. We have been able to demand information and we have been provided with that information. We are protected from silencing and interruptions and we are allowed to speak freely in the House.

However, the Opposition is not alone in effecting all this change; CCM members are increasingly becoming restless and discontent at their own party's control and are beginning to think and act above party interests. I want to highlight the fact that it is not just the Bunge that has been undergoing change. We could not have been able to do what we did if we were not supported by members of the ruling party who are like-minded, who believe that corruption regarding public finances is unacceptable and who share important information with other parties.

Other than that, the people of Tanzania are much more vocal and demanding than they used to be. This might be related to the fact that since 2006 all Bunge sessions are broadcast live on TV, paid for by Parliament. Before 2006 people could only listen to a short and edited fragment of the discussion in the Bunge over the radio. Now, and especially during the BoT and Richmond sessions, constituents call us after a difficult debate to tell us how we did.

The legislature is starting to take its oversight role more seriously, boosted by increasingly efficient committees, which are now using their investigative powers to expose issues that have caused the government much embarrassment. While it is still too early to claim a redefinition of the executive–legislative relationship, the Bunge is clearly becoming a viable guardian of the public interest.

12 The parliamentary public accounts committees in Nigerian states – structure, working practices and networking

Ben Ekeyi

The Nigerian public account committees

The public accounts committee (PAC) is the oldest and perhaps most influential committee in many of the world's parliaments. In Nigeria, the PAC is sometimes referred to as the 'mother of all committees'. The first Nigerian PAC was established in 1987 under the military regime of General Ibrahim Badamosi Babangida. The military leader appointed members of the Committee to work towards holding government accountable for the use of taxpayers' money. However, as there was no strong and direct accountability link (regular and free elections) between voters and military-appointed PAC members, the efficacy of the first PAC cannot, in any way, be compared to PACs operating in a democratic context. Furthermore, the military PAC's jurisdiction was limited only to the federal government and did not extend to the states. Despite this fact the existence of such a committee alludes to the importance of the PAC as an indispensible mechanism for instilling transparency and accountability in public finances.

The resuscitation of PACs[1] in Nigeria, during and after the advent of democracy in 1999, has proved very challenging. This is due to the fact that there were no records of past work done and there were no functional secretariats or experienced personnel to handle the crucial duties of the committees. However, over time the PACs have increasingly been able to increase their effectiveness. In fact, apart from the parliamentary PACs, some states, e.g. Lagos, have established executive-controlled PACs, whose function is to scrutinize the executive's finances prior to the scrutiny these records will receive from the parliamentary PAC. However, despite the proliferation of PACs, many regional PACs (State Houses of Assembly PACs) have a poor record of undertaking substantive activities. This is mainly because of the lack of funding available to them, executive interference and a lack of networking/coordination among the PACs, which would have enabled them to share ideas and learn from one another.

All PACs in Nigeria work very closely with the auditor-general's (AGs) office to ensure transparency and accountability in the financial operations of government at state and/or local level. In some states, there is an auditor-general for local governments appointed to look solely at local government finances and report his/her findings to Parliament. This chapter considers the PACs of eight Nigerian States: Abia, Bauchi, Benue, Cross River, Kaduna, Lagos, Niger and Sokoto. These states were selected in order to include a PAC from all the six geopolitical regions of Nigeria. Furthermore, the selection, within these regions, was random in order to ensure the inclusion of both relatively 'efficient' and 'not-so-efficient' PACs.

This chapter critically reviews the following aspects of PACs:

1   The role of PACs in ensuring accountability
2   The structure and working practices of Nigerian state PACs
3   The benefit of networking among PACs – the establishment of the National Council of Nigerian PACs
4   The role of the World Bank in strengthening state PACs in Nigeria

Public account committees and executive accountability

Governments all over the world, whether at the federal, state/provincial or local level, are faced with the problem of limited resources (taxpayer money) coupled with the expectations of citizens for high quality and effective delivery of public services. Citizens want to see that government provides all the services that make life meaningful for them. This is where the parliament comes in as a key institution in monitoring service delivery for all citizens through oversight. Oversight is carried out mainly through the sector-based committees in Parliament but most importantly through the PACs. PACs are responsible for ensuring that resources are used effectively, in a manner that would improve the quality of life of citizens and minimize the incidence of corruption and public-sector financial mismanagement.

The Nigerian Constitution stipulates that members of the executive are collectively and individually accountable to and must regularly provide comprehensive reports regarding the performance of their functions to the legislature. Sections 125 (4), (5), 128 (1b), (2b) and 129 (1a-d) of the Constitution all specifically require state legislatures to provide for effective mechanisms of oversight and to ensure that executive organs at the state level are held accountable to the legislatures. This legal framework, therefore, calls for a strong and virile parliament with an effective committee system. In 2001 the Commonwealth Parliamentary Association recognized that effective parliamentary oversight depends on the existence of an active committee system within legislatures. The PACs, and indeed all other sector-based committees in the legislature, must be adequately resourced to perform this important task of transparency and accountability. However, this objective can only be realized if PAC members and support staff have a clear understanding of the following:

1   The legislative environment and legal framework in which they operate;
2   The concept, principle and ethics of oversight and accountability;
3   The activities involved in the implementation of the oversight process;
4   The public-sector financial system;
5   The relationship between the PAC, other committees and stakeholders like the AG, attorney-general, anti-corruption agencies etc;
6   The need for measurement and evaluation in the context of the implementation of the oversight.

Research has shown that societies in which accountability is an integral part of public life experience higher levels of public confidence in government. There is no doubt that the quantity of direct investment, trade and economic growth is directly influenced by a state's reputation for good governance practices. To what extent are Nigerian PACs ready to provide effective oversight? The key criteria/key questions the PACs must ask are:

1   How has the work of PACs in the states improved public-sector governance and how can their work be further improved?
2   How can oversight be improved through effective follow-ups on audit queries and responses to reports?
3   How can greater service delivery be achieved through increased focus on value for money and performance audit?
4   What are the needs of state PACs and how can they be strengthened and supported?
5   How can state PACs share knowledge and experience in order for them to perform better?

The desire for greater efficiency, better performance, a service-orientated culture and outcomes-driven management by governments has highlighted the interrelationship between the work done by the various ministries and government departments, at all three spheres of government, and has accentuated the need for closer cooperation. Furthermore, there is also a need for PACs to learn from each other, especially considering their various unique working environments.

A democratic government is critically dependent on transparency and accountability to maintain its legitimacy. The main responsibility for achieving this task is in the hands of the legislatures. When legislatures oversee and scrutinize the actions of the executive effectively, they help to enforce government accountability and encourage high standards of ethical practice in the public sector, leading to efficient usage of public resources. There is, therefore, a need for strong parliamentary oversight and scrutiny guidelines as an essential part of promoting good governance.

Today there is a global trend towards greater openness in governments' financial management, and all over the world there are calls to strengthen public accountability and to re-examine how transparency and good governance can best be achieved. This is why societies and governments should work together in this task. Nigerian state PACs must accept and be part of this trend if they want to ensure transparency and accountability in their states.

The structure and working practices of Nigerian state PACs

The advent of democratic government in 1999 strengthened the legislature and established its presence as the most important component of the new democratic process. Committees are therefore important elements in every Nigerian parliament as they serve as the 'engine room' of the legislature. The PAC is one such committee. This section provides a baseline study of current PAC practices in Nigeria.

The section presents the results of a comparative analysis of the working practices of PACs across eight Nigerian states (Abia, Bauchi, Benue, Cross River, Kaduna, Lagos, Niger and Sokoto). The results of this research confirm the widely held opinion that Westminster style mechanisms for *ex-post* scrutiny are relatively robust. This is due to: (1) the quality of audit reports received by the committee from the auditor-general's office; and (2) the mutually beneficial relationship that exists between them (PACs and the AG's Office).

The structure, responsibilities and working practices of the PACs have been influenced by a number of factors, including:

1   Uniformity of the legislative base;
2   Differences and similarities in structure and working practices in the respective PAC jurisdictions;
3   The relationship between the PAC and the AG's office;
4   The role of subcommittees.

In short, while there are similarities in structure and terms of reference there are also variations in the working practices of the PACs.

Establishment and authority

The first PAC in Nigeria was established in 1987 under a military regime. With the advent of democracy in 1999, parliamentary PACs were re-established, albeit facing considerable challenges. In particular, new PACs faced the following challenges: (1) a lack of record keeping; and (2) no functional secretariats or experienced personnel to handle the crucial responsibilities of the PAC.

All the PACs in all the jurisdictions involved in this chapter are single independent 'standing committees' authorized to function via a legislative base. The major legislations that support their establishment are the 1999 Constitution of the Federal Republic of Nigeria and the various Rules of the Houses.

Generally all the PACs in Nigeria (except Lagos) reported enjoying an unrestricted right to investigate all government expenditures with an unrestricted right to access government agencies within and outside the Ministry of Finance. Following recent developments in public financial management, PACs have widened the scope of public audit practices to include private organizations and non-governmental organizations (NGOs), which have some financial dealings with the government. This is why, for example, the Sokoto State House of Assembly PAC reported having the right of access to private-sector organizations that have 'financial cum business transactions with MDAs'. Each PAC has the power to choose the subjects it investigates, make recommendations and publish conclusions without government interference.

Roles and responsibilities

All Nigerian state PACs have a responsibility to work closely with the auditor-general's office to ensure transparency and accountability in the financial operations of government at the state and local levels. This is done through the examination of the auditor-general's report submitted to the PACs via Parliament. The success of the PACs hinges on the effectiveness of the auditor-general's office since the bulk of inquiries emanate from that office. There are some variations in the powers PACs possess to undertake inquiries referred to them by the auditor-general and to initiate inquiries. For instance, all the PACs except Cross River, Kaduna and Lagos are empowered to initiate inquiries. Also, all have *ex-post* and *ex-ante* scrutiny powers with only slight variations.

In Nigeria, the State Houses of Assembly have little or nothing to do with the appointment of the auditor-general, which is usually the sole prerogative of the executive. Only two PAC jurisdictions, Kaduna and Lagos, must be formally consulted regarding the appointment of the auditor-general. None of the PACs are involved or make recommendations in the selection process. However, most of the jurisdictions have the power to veto the appointment and must be consulted before the AG's removal.

Membership and leadership

Several factors influence the structure of PAC membership in the Nigerian state houses of assembly. These factors include party representation in the parliament, size of the parliament, house rules/standing orders and existing conventions. Sokoto state's PAC has the highest number of members (11) while Benue has the lowest (3). Others have an average of seven members. Abia and Niger states have the highest number of opposition members on the PAC. However, overall, the ruling party has a majority of members on the PACs. Analysts have observed that this may not generate optimum results from the PACs as the ruling party members will always have their say and way even if the chair is an opposition party member.

Members of the PAC are normally appointed, for the term of parliament, by the leadership of the House via the Selection Committee. This is, however, subject to dissolution/reorganization by the leadership of the House at any time. It is pertinent to note that longevity of membership is believed to assist in strengthening the PAC.

Four of the eight PAC jurisdictions are chaired by opposition members – a fact in accord with the tradition among most PACs in the Commonwealth. It is generally believed that an opposition chair ensures better transparency in the work of the PAC. However, as a result of the challenges of democracy in Nigeria, it is often said that a chair from a government party will ensure that the PAC's views are better presented to the executive. Generally, the chairs are independent of party pressures and enjoy additional powers providing additional credibility to PAC reports.

Nature and sources of inquiry

There are significant differences in the nature and sources of PAC inquiries. It is generally accepted that the bulk of the PAC's work is dedicated to dealing with the auditor-general's reports. As stated earlier, the auditor-general's report is usually presented to Parliament, which then refers the report to the PAC for scrutiny. This explains why Parliament and the auditor-general's office are mutually dependent partners in the task of ensuring accountability in government spending. Usually, time constraints force the PACs to limit their work to those accounts involving a qualified audit opinion.

Most PACs in the state houses of assembly in Nigeria did not report an appreciable level of success in the number of inquiries, public hearings and meetings held per year. This is because of the following reasons:

1   Late submission of audit reports;
2   Submission of backlogs of reports all at once;
3   Inadequate staffing of the committees;
4   Untrained secretariat staff;
5   Poor knowledge of public sector financial system;
6   Inability to form quorum at meetings.

Only two out of the eight PACs (Abia and Kaduna) held an appreciable number of hearings per year, the average number being approximately seven. For most PACs, the volume of work available determines the number of meetings, but the average number for all jurisdictions is approximately five meetings.

Working Practices

PACs are normally very busy committees and members usually face heavy workloads, in addition to their regular legislative duties. Although subcommittees are not widely used in Nigeria, they can provide a solution to the heavy workload associated with PACs. Thus all the four PACs which reported possessing a subcommittee stated that they had been created to carry out substantive investigations and specific administrative duties. Also, as a result of time and resources limitations, PACs in Nigerian state houses of assembly give priority to inquiries based on:

1   The significance or potential significance of the matter for the reputation of the state;
2   The calibre of persons involved in the allegations;
3   The credibility of the allegations the PAC is investigating;
4   The sum of money involved;
5   The level of public concern;
6   Whether the issue could be referred to another existing standing or select committee in the House.

Deliberative meetings are not open to the public but hearings are open unless the PAC determines to take evidence in camera, which rarely occurs. In conducting inquiries, the majority of PACs have considerable power to summon diverse witnesses and access documents, a power which has been identified across the Commonwealth as being very important for the success of PACs. Generally, PACs call on the commissioners rather than the accounting officers of the MDAs to appear before the PAC.

The PAC's ability to efficiently and effectively undertake inquiries is also largely dependent on the availability of its members and the level/quality of its staff available for the committee. A typical PAC in Nigeria has an average of six full-time staff with occasional support staff from the auditor-general's office. Sokoto State has the highest number of staff members (7) while Benue has the lowest (1). The bulk of the committee's staff work is basically the preparation of reports after the scrutiny of the auditor-general's audit report, committee reports, record keeping, data processing and other administrative duties.

In drafting PAC reports, all states reviewed in this chapter stated that the report/findings are usually drafted by the Committee secretary/clerk with the assistance of the secretariat staff. The report is, however, sent to the Committee chair and other members for vetting before being tabled in Parliament. All reports tabled in Parliament are subject to debates by parliamentarians and the duration and frequency of these debates are a function of the volume of reports produced by the PAC. Frequent debating of the PAC report on the floor of the House will raise the profile of audit reports and increase the pressure on government to actually implement recommendations.

Monitoring the implementation of audit inquiry recommendations has proven very challenging for PACs all over the world. State house of assembly PACs are no exception to this rule. A vast majority of state PACs in Nigeria reported that monitoring of the implementation of PAC recommendations is usually through external actors, mainly the auditor-general's office and sometimes via the oversight functions of sector-based committees in the House. This has assisted in getting the government to accept and implement recommendations promptly but it has not been sufficient. The UK Hansard Society has suggested that 'Departmental Annual Reports' should have a section solely dedicated to the progress made in implementing recommendations and the result of the changes made. In Ghana, the Parliament has passed a bill to withhold allocations to erring MDAs. This has proven very effective and can be duplicated in Nigerian states.

Capacity-building, both for parliamentarians and staff, is an urgent necessity among state PACs in Nigeria. Since the advent of democracy in 1999, Nigerian PACs have battled with poor working conditions and inexperienced staff and members.

Performance disclosure and evaluation

In Nigeria, most state PACs do not have formal mechanisms for evaluating their performance. Only Kaduna and Sokoto reported having a formal mechanism but these have not been effectively utilized. Though annual reports are issued, the majority of PACs do not disclose quantifiable performance information, such as key performance indicators (KPIs). This makes it impossible for the PAC to actually assess its performance and seek to improve where necessary.

None of the eight state PACs reviewed has had any contact with other PACs. Study visits, tours and exchange of ideas are not encouraged amongst the PACs. This isolated status has not helped individual PACs to improve as there is no exchange of experiences. The only time two or more PACs meet is at conferences or seminars and this is usually informal. As a result, the resuscitation of the idea of a Nigerian Council of PACs became a reality.

The establishment of the National Council of Nigerian PACs

The need to facilitate PAC effectiveness through networking has raised the demand for the formation of the National Council of Nigerian PACs (NCNPACs). The inception the NCNPAC can be traced to 2001. In July of that year some national parliamentarians at a joint meeting of both the House of Representatives and Senate PACs resolved that there should be an association of PACs in Nigeria. The association was to comprise both the state house of assembly PACs and those of the National Assembly (the Senate and House of Representatives). This resolution was backed by an action plan designed to make the state PACs aware of the rationale behind the formation of such an association.

In 2004, a Public Financial Management Conference was organized in Kaduna. The idea of a national association of PACs was again brought to the limelight. All speakers at the conference agreed that there was a need for such an association with the objective of helping bring all PACs together and foster unity, and the dissemination of best practices and procedures amongst the committees. As a result, the conference resolved to found the association with the National Assembly spearheading the initiative. Unfortunately, the idea was dropped once the participants departed from the conference.

As a result, PACs in various jurisdictions continued to function independently without any form of networking. This lack of coordination was partly responsible for the poor performance amongst Nigerian state PACs, which became almost fused into the executive arm of government. Consequently the overall public financial management in Nigeria was adversely affected, with corruption thriving in the states.

The WBI intervenes

The World Bank via the World Bank Institute has supported the idea of establishing the Nigerian Council of Public Accounts Committees (NCPACs). This support was evident when, in partnership with the Commonwealth Parliamentary Association and Parliamentary Centre, the World Bank Institute organized a five-day seminar entitled 'Africa Regional Public Accounts Committee (PAC) Seminar' from 1–5 March, 2009 in Accra, Ghana. The seminar was organized with the following aims:

1   Enhancing the knowledge of members of parliament, senior professional parliamentary staff and representatives from supreme audit institutions on issues related to effective financial oversight;
2   Strengthening the working relationship between parliaments and their corresponding national audit institutions;
3   Sharing experiences and learning lessons on best practices from member states;
4   Building networks and enhancing collaboration among member states;

After thorough sessions of papers and jurisdiction experience discussions, including a paper on the need for an association of PACs in Nigeria, the participating states resolved to ensure the foundation of an association that would enable PACs to coordinate and share their experiences.

The journey so far

Departing from the seminar with the above resolutions/action plans, the four participating Nigerian state PACs began the process of establishing the network by mobilizing other states in their respective geopolitical regions. The Nigerian association is likened to existing provincial association of PACs like the Association of Public Accounts Committees in South Africa. So far, the pioneering states have only succeeded in establishing a working structure for the association. Unfortunately, this structure has not functioned effectively due in part to funding constraints and due to the lack of focus by parliamentarians in the face of pending elections in 2011. Despite these setbacks it is hoped that a renewed focus on setting up the association will resume after the elections.

Conclusion

Since the re-establishment of democracy in Nigeria it has become increasingly possible for the executive's financial activities to be subject to oversight by the legislature, at the local, state and national level via PACs. However, despite their proliferation, Nigerian state PACs suffer from a number of constraints, poor incentive mechanisms and a lack of coordination, which limit their oversight effectiveness. Nigerian PACs will only be able to reach their full potential if they are able to operate independently of the executive, have access to well-trained staff and can coordinate with each other in order to identify and benefit from the proliferation of best practices.

Note

1   At the federal level, there are two PACs, one in the House of Representatives and one in the Senate.

13 Role model for the world

The formation of the African
Parliamentarians Network
Against Corruption (APNAC)
and its regional and
global impact

Given Lubinda

How was APNAC Founded?

The African Parliamentarians Network Against Corruption (APNAC) was founded in February 1999 at a Regional Seminar on the theme 'Parliament and Good Governance' held in Kampala, Uganda. Thirty parliamentarians representing each African region participated at the week-long seminar. This diverse body of attendees ensured that a wide variety of experiences, relating to different strategies for combating corruption, were shared and discussed. This process of information-sharing convinced many of the participants of the usefulness of exchanging information and experiences about the fight against corruption, as the process helped identify best practices and new strategies that might work in their respective countries. Consequently, the conference participants felt the need to build upon their experience by maintaining contact with each other as well as reaching out to parliamentarians and parliamentary organizations throughout Africa. Thus, they decided to establish APNAC.

Once the decision to establish APNAC was taken, arrangements were soon put in place to try and ensure its long-term sustainability. The Hon. Augustine Ruzindana (then chair of Uganda's Public Accounts Committee) was elected as chair of the Interim Coordinating Committee and the Hon. Lindiwe Zulu (Deputy Speaker of the Gauteng Provincial Legislature) was elected vice chair with support of representatives from Benin, Ghana, Kenya, Mozambique, Tanzania and Zimbabwe, ensuring that a diverse range of views from all the regions and countries of the continent were involved right from the genesis of APNAC.

Chronologically, the key milestone events surrounding APNAC's formation were:

1   *The first APNAC Newsletter* (March 1999) – built momentum by demonstrating the potential of the network by: (1) providing APNAC members with information regarding the objectives of the network; as well as (2) media reaction to APNAC's creation; (3) disseminating the findings of reports, by members, on their follow-up activities; and (4) providing information on subsequent international anti-corruption initiatives of interest to members.
2   *Video-Conference Meeting* (July 1999) – allowed participants at the Laurentian Seminar on Parliamentary Accountability and the Control of Corruption Part II to share findings and conclusions of the First Seminar with counterparts in the Ugandan and Tanzanian Parliaments as well as to plan the next steps in the development of APNAC.
3   *The drafting of APNAC's Constitution* (completed October, 1999): took place at the meeting of the Ninth International Anti-Corruption Conference (IACC) in Durban, South Africa. The rationale behind the selection of this location was that APNAC could take advantage of the attendance of over 100 African MPs – including many APNAC members – as well as the presence of numerous academics and practitioners. APNAC hosted a workshop on the 'Role of Parliamentarians in Curbing Corruption'. After the workshop the first annual meeting of the APNAC Coordination Committee was convened, which finalized: (a) the draft APNAC Constitution; (b) the details on the establishment of a secretariat; (c) the establishment of national chapters in Benin, Ghana, Kenya, South Africa, Uganda and Zimbabwe; and, (d) the launching of the APNAC website (http://www.apnac.org).
4   *The establishment of a Secretariat* (completed January 2000): initially based in Kampala (Uganda), but now in Accra (Ghana).

Membership and governance

There are three critical institutions that constitute the core of APNAC. These are: (1) the national chapters; (2) the secretariat; and, (3) the executive council.

National chapters

The 19 member countries of APNAC are Benin, Burkina Faso, Cameroon, Chad, The Democratic Republic of Congo, the Gambia, Ghana,

Kenya, Malawi, Mali, Niger, Nigeria, Rwanda, Senegal, Sierra Leone, Tanzania, Uganda, Zambia and Zimbabwe. Each member country has its own 'national chapter'. These national chapters (NCs) operate on a non-profit, non-partisan and non-governmental basis, and have their own constitutions. While the specific activities of each NC reflect the needs of the country, they have broadly similar objectives, which include:

1 The commitment to build the capacity of MPs to exercise accountability and effective oversight of the executive (especially with respect to financial matters);
2 To establish a legal framework to ensure appropriate funding of political parties and free, transparent, fair and credible elections;
3 To mobilize internal and external resources to support anti-corruption projects;
4 To promote legislation that would allow information dissemination and give the media the means to inform the public on the holdings and liabilities of public officials and political leaders;
5 To share information on lessons learned and best practices.

The secretariat

The APNAC secretariat's role is to support, coordinate and maintain cross-national linkages between the national chapters. Specifically, the secretariat:

1 Keeps records of membership, including national chapters, and promotes new membership and affiliations;
2 Coordinates and facilitates the activities of the various organs of the organization and, in particular, supports the executive council;
3 Collects and disseminates information concerning the organization and its members and national chapters;
4 Assists in the formation of national chapters;
5 Ensures that the organization's membership is well informed about its programmes and activities;
6 Maintains liaison and co-ordinates activities between the organization and other groups or institutions;
7 Coordinates the organization's representation and conferences;
8 Handles finances, keeps the records and archives of the organization;
9 Is the HQ of the organization.

The executive council

APNAC is governed by an elected, gender-inclusive executive council, composed of a chair, vice-chair, and two representatives from each of the four regions of Africa – Central, Eastern, Southern and Western. Each national chapter has its own chair and vice-chair. At the time of writing, the executive council was composed of:

1   President: Hon. Given Lubinda (MP, Zambia)
2   Vice-President: Hon. Dieudonné Maurice Bonanet (MP, Burkina Faso)
3   Central Africa: Hon. Ouchar Tourgoudi (MP, Chad)
4   Central Africa: Dr Bouzabo Patchili (MP, Chad)
5   East Africa: Hon. Musikari Kombo (MP, Kenya)
6   East Africa: Hon. Dr Zainab Amir Gama (MP, Tanzania)
7   Southern Africa: Hon. Eduardo Namburete (MP, Mozambique)
8   Southern Africa: Hon. Jabulani Mangena (MP, Zimbabwe)

Partners and Collaborators

Apart from its governance structure (as presented above), APNAC also works with and/or is supported by a number of agencies and organizations, namely:

(i)   The Canadian International Development Agency (CIDA): APNAC has benefited from CIDA support through the Parliamentary Centre's Africa–Canada Parliamentary Strengthening Program (ACPSP). For example, between 2002 and 2007, CIDA provided APNAC with support in order to strengthen the capacity of democratic African parliaments to: (1) increase transparency in decision-making; (2) achieve effective parliamentary oversight and accountability through anti-corruption efforts, poverty reduction strategies and gender-equality actions; and (3) participate in the effective and inclusive implementation of the New Partnership for Africa's Development (NEPAD).

(ii) The Danish International Development Agency (DANIDA): DANIDA recently provided a grant to APNAC. In the context of this partnership, APNAC sees the new funding being provided by the DANIDA as a very welcome and useful complement to the present work being done to strengthen the capacity of the network, expand national chapters, and increase parliamentary efforts against corruption. The funding will be used in ways that will respect and strengthen the results framework within the different components of support for which DANIDA is providing assistance.

(iii) Parliamentary Centre: APNAC and the Parliamentary Centre have worked closely together since the formation of the network in 1999. In April 2003, a formal partnership agreement was signed between the two organizations in Addis Ababa with the aim of cooperating in order to ensure the implementation of the CIDA-funded Africa–Canada Parliamentary Strengthening Program (ACPSP). This agreement went on to state that, 'This program seeks to strengthen accountability, transparency, representational equity and policy impact from democratic parliaments in governance in Africa.' More specifically, the ACPSP aims to strengthen democratic parliaments in Africa via three African parliamentary networks: on poverty reduction, gender equality and anti-corruption, which share best practices and connect better with the New Partnership for Africa's Development (NEPAD).

(iv) Transparency International (TI): one of the world's leading anti-corruption policy groups, TI has been a strong supporter of APNAC since the network was created. Apart from participation at APNAC's conferences and activities, several TI chapters in Africa have formed partnerships with national APNAC chapters in which they serve as the secretariat of the latter e.g. the TI chapters in Kenya, Tanzania and Zimbabwe.

The support provided by these partners has been critical for APNAC's development. As and when APNAC required the expertise and resources in order to carry out its activities, these organizations were able to provide it. Despite this support, some projects continue to be delayed or are more limited in scope than would be optimal, because of the financial and technical constraints that continue to affect APNAC.

Functions and activities

The main objectives of APNAC are to:

1 Build the commitment of parliaments to exercise accountability, with emphasis on financial matters;
2 Share information and best practices;
3 Undertake projects to control corruption;
4 Sensitize, educate and raise awareness among the population of the existence, threat and danger of corruption;

5   Advocate for inclusion of corruption issues in government priority programmes;
6   Advocate for and encourage improvement of state capacity to address and handle matters related to corruption in a timely way;
7   Liaise with national and international organizations (including civil society) and institutions on all matters of corruption;
8   Mobilize internal and external resources to promote anti-corruption programmes;
9   Develop links with other oversight committees of parliament and parliamentarians across Africa.

APNAC achieves its objectives via several channels. Firstly, the existence of the APNAC newsletter provides members of the network with information regarding: (1) the experiences of other members; and (2) global developments and best practices in the fight against corruption. Secondly, APNAC national chapters play a critical role in tailoring this information into effective anti-corruption strategies that are suitable to the specific country/regional context in which they operate. Thus, for example, Chad's APNAC chapter participated in the formulation and adoption of two laws on management of public goods, while Kenya's APNAC chapter, in association with Transparency International and the Friedrich Ebert Stiftung (FES), developed a case study of the expenditure patterns of MPs in different parts of the country in order to gain a better understanding of the magnitude and importance of patron–client relationships in African politics.

Finally, APNAC itself has sought to facilitate knowledge dissemination and value added by supporting a host of activities. APNAC has run numerous seminars and conferences e.g. APNAC has participated in annual conferences such as the annual 'Anti Money Laundering Conference' and the 'Global Forum on Anti-Corruption'. APNAC has also run numerous specialist workshops that either focus on specific pressing issues such as recently organized workshops on Public Procurement (in Ghana and Kenya), and Political Corruption (in Uganda). It has also undertaken a regional Training of Trainers (ToT) workshop for a number of MPs from English-speaking countries as well as an Anti-Corruption training workshop for Eastern and Southern Africa chapters. The APNAC secretariat has also been instrumental in supporting the establishment and the visitations (for revitalization purposes) of national chapters in order to provide support and build momentum for national anti-corruption activities (e.g. the launch of APNAC's Liberian chapter in July 2007 and recent visits by the APNAC president and executive director to chapters in Eastern and Western Africa, including some francophone countries).

Challenges

In the 11 years since its foundation, APNAC has managed to increase its numerical strength as well as the scope of its activities. This is despite the fact that during the first years after its inception APNAC suffered from a severe lack of funding – with almost all the activities planned in 2001/2002 either not implemented or scaled down due to these fiscal constraints. Apart from the central issue of financial constraints, APNAC faces the following ongoing challenges:

1 The endemic problem of political instability: while the level of political instability varies by country, APNAC activities have sometimes been disrupted by pressing political concerns. For example, the national chapter in Uganda reported that during the 2006 elections many of its members as well as the nation's media lost sight of the importance of a sustained anti-corruption effort, as the focus shifted to short-term campaign concerns. This had the unintended effect of derailing several anti-corruption initiatives. Furthermore, some national chapters have reported that it is difficult to engage with key stakeholders due to deep partisan divides and suspicions that render cross-party dialogue and consensus on anti-corruption measures usually difficult, if not impossible, to develop and sustain.

2 Loss of communication with members and the need to continually establish new contacts: while democratic turnover is an essential prerequisite in the fight against corruption, the fact that APNAC has to continuously strive to establish new contacts, given the financial constraints it faces, poses a significant operational challenge for the organization.

3 Funding of projects at the national level: more than one national chapter has reported that its ability to effectively implement planned anti-corruption activities has been constrained by the lack of funds.

Despite these persistent constraints, APNAC has managed to sustain and eventually increase its anti-corruption role via the activities it facilitates as well as the increase in its national chapters.[1]

APNAC and GOPAC

Perhaps one of the biggest contributions APNAC has made to the fight against corruption is the successful 'export' of its modus operandi to the rest of the world. By demonstrating the potential benefits of an anti-corruption network of parliamentarians, APNAC has shown what could be achieved by bringing committed MPs together to fight corruption. Therefore, when, at a 2002 global conference of parliamentarians in Ottawa, Canadian John Williams (MP) spearheaded the process that would result in the founding of the Global Organization of Parliamentarians Against Corruption (GOPAC – registered as a Charity in 2003), it was possible to use APNAC's structure as a basis for organizing GOPAC's institutions. In fact, GOPAC's organization, with its regional (now including APNAC) and national chapters, is in many ways a replica of APNAC at the global level.[2]

Conclusion

APNAC was founded in order to facilitate African parliamentarians' capability to share their experiences and methods of combating corruption in a systematic and cost-effective manner. Furthermore, APNAC's inclusiveness: (1) regional remit (no part of the continent was excluded); as well as (2) its emphasis on national and sub-national levels of engagement (founding of national chapters with constitutions tailored towards the need of a given country); means that it is capable of facilitating solutions that are context-specific and can be critically reviewed by grass-roots/local stakeholders. The success of APNAC is not just seen by the proliferation of national chapters and the work they do, but also by the development of GOPAC, whose modus operandi and aims are to replicate APNAC's success at the global level.

Notes

1   http://www.gopacnetwork.org/Docs/APNAC%20Paper%20-%20en.pdf.
2   http://www.gopacnetwork.org/AboutUs/faq_en.htm.

14 The growth of constituency development funds in Africa and beyond

Institutionalized rent-extraction or constituency-specific development assistance?

Mark Baskin and Rasheed Draman

This chapter explores the implications, for socio-economic development, of the existence of 'constituency development funds' (CDFs). By examining what factors determine the consequences of CDFs the chapter identifies the conditions under which CDFs are likely to be a driver for locally focused development or, conversely, fuel rent-seeking and rent-extraction by politicians and interest groups. This critical appraisal of CDFs is achieved via two sections. First, the general discussion of CDFs, by Mark Baskin, analyzes the controversies surrounding CDFs and how the context (governance structure) they are embedded in is critical in determining whether they are a driver of development or corruption. This analysis is made more concrete in the second section of the chapter, in which Rasheed Draman critically examines the operation of CDFs in Ghana, a case study that demonstrates empirically how critical the governance context is in determining the consequences of the existence and operation of CDFs.

Constituency development funds in the abstract

What are consistency development funds?

Constituency development funds (CDFs) is the generic name for a policy tool that dedicates public money to benefit specific political subdivisions through allocations and/or spending decisions influenced by the political subdivision's representatives in the national parliament. In short CDFs represent a form of redistributive politics and policymaking, which have the potential of being policy tools that can fuel decentralized development, moving decisions from the centre of policymaking (a one-size-fits-all modus operandi) to sub-national districts (sub-national needs modi operandi).

As economies in the 'developing world' grow and their political systems become increasingly stable, CDFs have become increasingly popular. They are found in a growing and diverse set of developing countries, such as Kenya, Bhutan, Jamaica and Papua New Guinea, as well as in the distributive politics (generally called 'pork barrel') in US national and state level policymaking.

Why are consistency development funds controversial?

Operations of CDFs remain controversial in donor communities because they raise fundamental questions about democratic theory, the efficacy of government service delivery, the extent to which such service delivery can be made accountable, the role of legislators in selecting development priorities, and how public participation in policymaking can be made more meaningful.

Enhanced transparency appears to require a separation and balance of powers. A CDF that is centrally controlled by the executive (as previously in Ghana) and is strictly accountable to the president or prime minister may leave little room for transparency in its operations. However, it would seem relatively simple to enhance transparency in CDF operations that would lead to more effective accountability of CDFs – either through legislation expanding freedom of information and/or enhancing the increasing transparency and openness of government administration more fully.

The role of consistency development funds in fostering development

CDFs are becoming increasingly significant tools of politicized and decentralized resource allocation in developing countries. They are popular (even in the US!) in the face of a donor community that continues to prefer traditional development that is driven by central governments in a manner that resembles 'rationality' in economically advanced and powerful nations. The CDFs are evolving quickly and are emerging as increasingly important development tools. Their popularity may stem from their performance of a function not otherwise supplied by the existing administrative-political system. As in the case of earmarks in the US, CDFs could fill the holes for things that fall between the cracks. However, the enormous potential for abuse in the operations of CDFs creates a significant challenge for policymakers and scholars to devise norms, rules and procedures for the effective operation of these increasingly important policy tools.

Benchmarks of success: what does the evidence say?

The vast corpus of research in institutional economics and the development and evolution of CDFs suggests that how these funds are administered is critical in determining whether they foster meaningful local development or simply generate pork-barrel and rent-extraction opportunities for public policymakers and interest groups. Specifically, deficiencies in the following variables/governance mechanisms are likely to result in limited welfare gains, for the average citizen, of the operation of CDFs:

1   Accountability and transparency deficiencies resulting from the lack of a clear, effective mechanism for oversight or separation of powers delineated in CDF policy, can lead to:

   a   *Unaccounted for or wasted money* because balance sheets are improperly, dishonestly or rarely reported.
   b   *Corruption* when MPs use funds to buy political favours or votes; when decentralized levels of government, administration and civil society organisations fail to maintain and submit to central CDF administration detailed records of money used; and/or project designers or implementers are selected on the basis of clientelism or nepotism.
   c   *Disillusioned constituencies* because they were not consulted at any or all stages of project identification, proposal, selection, approval and implementation.

2   Efficiency issues arise when there is a misallocation, misuse or underutilization of CDF disbursements as a consequence of:

   a   *Fiscal illusion,* or the inability of local populations to grasp the aggregate cost of all CDF projects for the central government and its impact on the national budget. In this case, because CDF money does not come directly from a constituency's revenue or tax base, it is treated as 'free money', diminishing the degree of efficient utilization of and effort to monitor such disbursements. Also, the central government incurs the long-term cost of these projects, which is a hidden cost.
   b   *Project duplication* with development efforts of national and local government or development efforts funded by the donor community.

   c *Poorly designed projects* due to the lack of a coherent policy framework within which to propose, devise and implement projects, which ultimately promotes waste.

   d *Incompetent administration* in local government that may be technically ill equipped to administer project funds due to the technical complexity of management practice.

3 Equity dilemmas surface partly because of different approaches to defining three core elements of what is meant by 'fair CDF distribution'. To address these three elements, one must define who the deserving *recipients* are, what the limits are of the *project or item* for which money is allocated and how you gauge the fairness of the *process* of distribution.

The general controversies and challenges surrounding the development of CDFs can be better understood and evaluated with respect to a specific case. By examining the development, operation and evolution of CDFs in Ghana it becomes obvious that the governance mechanisms that CDFs operate in are the critical determinant for whether CDFs ultimately foster local development, are rendered ineffectual or, in the worst case, become a vehicle for rent-extraction and pork-barrel politics.

A case study of the development of the constituency development fund in Ghana

Background

The District Assemblies Common Fund, Ghana's hybrid form of CDFs, like most redistributive policies in Africa, has a history that is linked to colonialism; a history of centralization of power and distribution of resources. This practice, which created enclaves of 'haves' and 'have-nots' within Ghanaian society, continued beyond colonialism. Long after colonialism and independence, the practice persists and is perpetuated by the often bitter, partisan and winner-takes-all politics that has come to characterize political competition in Ghana, as in many other African countries.

It is often the practice that communities that are seen as anti-government or hotbeds of opposition suffer from lack of development and infrastructural development, decisions about which are often made from the 'centre'. All this 'top-down' and skewed allocation of resources has done is to ensure that certain parts of the country are better than others.

In an effort to correct these historical 'mistakes' and undo this colonial and post-colonial legacy, the country took a bold step in 1988 by promulgating the District Assemblies Law. The law decentralized political and economic governance of the country by creating 110 Districts that were to be 'centres of local governance'. Among other things, the law:

1   Sought to achieve the goal of ensuring participation, effectiveness and accountability development through local governance;
2   Created local assemblies in all districts to help achieve this key goal as well as give people a voice in their own development; and
3   Created the position of district chief executive – to be appointed by the president; 70 per cent of the members of the assembly elected and 30 per cent appointed by the president. This political structure was the vehicle through which decentralization and redistribution would find meaning.

The biggest pitfall of the law was this political structure described above. Critics argue that what the law did was to reorganize 'centralization' of authority by simply creating a 'centralized' system within a 'decentralized' structure, given that the key decision-maker and political head of the district, as well one third of the assembly, is appointed at the top and owes allegiance not to the people they represent, but to the president and power brokers at the 'centre' of political authority. By so doing, it appeared the architects of decentralization in Ghana were not sincere in crafting the law and were more interested in holding on to political authority and power than in decentralization.

After creating the political structure through which to deliver decentralization, the issue of how to fund decentralization – resources to deliver 'the development goal' that is to be championed by local people – became the next most important question. As a result, fiscal decentralization thus became a key feature of the decentralization process. Fiscal power was, therefore, 'devolved' from the 'centre' to the local level, through the creation of the District Assemblies Common Fund (DACF) – a fund under which 'all things were to be possible', including funding 'pet projects' of members of parliament through what has become known as members of parliament share of the common fund – the Ghanaian version of the constituency development fund.

Structure of the fund

At the time the District Assemblies Law was passed in 1988, Ghana was under a military dictatorship so it is difficult to ascertain how transparent the process was at the time. It is possible that the debates, discussions and deliberations leading to the passage of the law were 'controlled' by the military regime of the time without much public input and participation. Even if there was public input, it is not clear how much of that was accepted by the military junta of the time.

As indicated earlier, an important issue in the Ghanaian decentralization process was fiscal decentralization. This was important to give district assemblies the financial resources that they need to deliver development.

According to the District Assemblies Common Fund Act, 1993, Act 455:

1   There shall be a fund to be known as the District Assemblies Common Fund referred to as 'the Common Fund';
2   The Common Fund shall consist of all monies allocated by Parliament under section 2 of the Act and any interests and dividends accruing from investments of monies from the Common Fund;

According to section 2 of the Act, 'Parliament shall annually allocate not less than five per cent of the total revenue of Ghana to the District Assemblies for development.' In 2008, the Common Fund allocation was increased from 5 per cent to 7.5 per cent of national revenue. Generally the 7.5 per cent of the national revenue goes into a pool that is distributed by the administrator of the fund to all district assemblies based on a number key factors, among them:

1   The need factor: to address current developmental imbalances;
2   The service pressure factor: to assist in improving existing services which, as a result of population pressure, are deteriorating;
3   The equalization factor: to ensure that each district has access to a specified minimum sum from the fund;
4   Reserve fund.

In distributing the Fund, the mathematical allocations are as follows:

1   District assemblies receive 90 per cent of the fund
2   10 per cent is kept in reserve, out of which:
3   5 per cent is shared equally among MPs (MPs' Common Fund) for constituency development projects;

4 2.5 per cent goes to regional coordinating councils – the governing bodies of the decentralized structures at the regional level;

5 0.5 per cent goes to the fund administrator for field operations; and

6 2 per cent is kept for contingency.

One notable change that took place was the fact that MPs' share of the fund increased to from 5 per cent to 6 per cent when the fund was increased from 5 per cent to 7.5 per cent in 2008.

MPs and the Fund

At the inception of the DACF, the role of Parliament was limited to its traditional function of oversight. This function is consistent with its core mandate as the principal watchdog of public expenditure and in particular countervailing the executive's power and authority to handle and spend public resources in the best interest of the citizens.

In 1998, after a decade of implementation of the National Decentralization Programme, the DACF, which is a form of devolution of control of resources to the local level, was reviewed. The review introduced a significant dimension of creating a share for members of parliament; a move that has since had implications on the essence of the concept and further deepened the politicization of development at the district level. As a supplemental source of funding for district development, the MPs' share of the DACF has had considerable electoral implications, especially, for the MPs whose constituents expect them to bring physical development. This is one of the main reasons for assigning a share of the fund to members of parliament to make tangible input into the development of districts.

As elected representatives of their constituencies,[1] MPs are viewed by the electorate as the main agents of development and are the first point of call for solutions to emergencies at both the district and community levels. This state of affairs has historical antecedence where elected representatives in the immediate post-independence era were, in the literal sense, among the few literate and capable facilitators of state–citizens dialogue and therefore the official medium of public-funded development at the district level. Members of constituencies look up to MPs for development projects instead of to DAs, which are well placed and better resourced as an extension of the executive. And interestingly the legislative function of an MP is least among the reasons for non-return of MPs after elections. Rather, the electoral fortunes of an MP depend, to a large extent, on the physical infrastructure he/she has influenced or helped bring to the constituency. In other words, citizens view MPs as development agents.

Against this background and the enormous demands placed on MPs to bring development to their constituencies, and the limitations they face in accessing funds both at the national and local levels, particularly if they are opposition MPs, they pushed for the review of the DACF in 1998. The primary aim of the review was to provide MPs with a privileged position as agents of district development through the introduction a share for them within the DACF.

Another motivation, apart from their political fortunes and personal self-interest, is the fact that it enables equitable spread of development projects to communities that may not have voted for the government in power at any point in time. This hidden reason relates closely to the argument that MPs are close to the grass roots and therefore appreciate the real needs of communities.

Access to the funds by MPs

Under the provisions of Article 252 of Ghana's 1992 Constitution, the DACF is set up as a mechanism for the transfer of resources from the central government to the local authorities – the metropolitan, municipal and district assemblies (MMDAs). The Article initially provided that 5 per cent of Ghana's total revenue should be paid into the fund for distribution to these local-level authorities, mainly to undertake development projects and some specific programmes. Subsequently, Parliament enacted the District Assemblies Common Fund Act (Act 455) in July 1993 to provide further legislation and detail on the administration of the fund. The distribution of the fund is based on a formula proposed by the by the administrator and approved by Parliament. In fact, according Article 7 of the Act:

1   The administrator has the following functions –

- To propose a formula annually for the distribution of the Common Fund for approval by Parliament;
- To administer and distribute monies paid into the Common Fund among the district assemblies in accordance with the formula approved by Parliament;
- To report in writing to the minister on how allocations made from the Common Fund to the district assemblies have been utilized by the district assemblies; and
- To perform any other functions that may be directed by the President.

To access the fund, MPs are expected to identify the projects they intend to apply the resources to, and such projects should be in tandem with priorities of the district assembly development priority. Upon MPs' submission of a proposal or memo with a budget to the district chief executive (DCE) requesting funds for specified projects, the DCE studies and signs the request to approve disbursement of funds for that purpose, thus authorizing the district coordinating director and the financial officer, who are signatories to the account, to prepare and sign the cheque.

Challenges faced by MPs

The accessing of the funds by MPs has, however, not been without controversy, even though the official procedure is clear. The MP is expected to identify a project and work within the district tender board to see the execution of the project. However, the implementation of projects with MPs' share of the DACF has not been without accountability challenges, as is indeed the case with DAs in the use of the fund. It is reported there are instances where MPs directly access their share of the funds and single-handedly decide on projects and beneficiary communities, make payments on procurements without recourse to district tender boards or the procurement rules.

As a result, staff of district assemblies are some of the strong proponents for the abolishing of the MPs' share of the DACF, with the explanation that the use of the fund is duplicating district development efforts and therefore wasteful of scarce resources. Not surprising, there are tensions between some district chief executives and their MPs when the former are suspected of harbouring ambitions to contest the parliamentary seat for the constituency. Consequently, undue delays and cases of non-use of funds allocated to some MPs have been reported. The friction is severe where the MP and the DCE are from different parties, and with that there have allegations of sabotage of MPs' projects through such delays and non-release of funds to the MP, to the detriment of the community.

With these challenges, some MPs are proposing that MPs should be cosignatories to the MPs' share of the fund, arguing that the present arrangement gives too much control of the fund to the district chief executive and the district assembly.

There are also concerns that the fund is woefully inadequate to effectively act as one of the main sources of funding for district development. This case is strengthened by the fact that most districts, particularly in areas already disadvantaged by severe geographic conditions or whose resources are yet to be greatly explored and exploited, are incapable of development without such transfers from the central government.

As a result of the reported abuses, the fund administrator, according to the pilot study referred to earlier, has initiated steps to curb the misappropriation of the fund. This includes recommendations for all payments to pass through the district assembly accounting system.

Transparency and accountability

With the launch of the national decentralization programme in 1988, the decentralized system has increasingly involved local government structures – the MMDAs in the administrative functions of government. Section 240 (2, c) of the Local Government Act, 1993 (Act 462) provides that each local government unit shall have a sound financial base with adequate and reliable sources of revenue. This is an emphasis on fiscal decentralization, one of the key considerations for the devolution of authority.

Despite this emphasis, if one carefully analyzes the decentralization processes and the structure of the DACF that has been set up, it is clear, ironically, that central government has been unwilling to cede control of financial resources to the MMDAs, and, in substantive ways, certain actions are centralizing rather than devolving power and resources to DAs.

There is reluctance on the part of central government agencies to decentralize the ministries and their proper integration at the district level. In the instance of the DACF, there are frequent delays in disbursement of the fund to MMDAs, mainly also because of delayed payment of funds into the fund, despite the constitutional status of the DACF and requirement of payments into the fund. In the implementation of the DACF, there is a very heavy centralization of resources and a requirement for the retention of some monies allocated by the fund administrator at the central level of government.

While amounts received by the DAs agree with allocations released from the office of the administrator of the DACF, official deductions at source in the form of 'capacity building of the DAs, bulk purchases of supplies for DAs, and contributions to the National Association of Local Governments (NALAG)' have often considerably reduced the value of the actual allocations to the DAs. Besides these deductions, official directives that accompany the releases guide the utilization of other 'earmarked funds' and these are often related to central government needs rather than needs at the local level.

Against these constraints on effective implementation of the DACF, the role of the DCE in the DAs is central to achieving accelerated decentralization. As an appointee of the executive, any meaningful review of the decentralization programme is expected to include making the DCE an elected official of the DA. This will significantly improve both administrative and fiscal decentralization. For one thing, the DCE will now be accountable to the people who elected him/her rather than to the president and other power structures at the central level of government. However, with the discretionary powers in the allocation of DACF (through deductions by the office of the fund administrator), coupled with the influence DCE's wield over the disbursement of the MPs' share of the fund, the subject continues to be only speculation.

With the strong central control of the DACF compounded by the compromising interest of MPs through their share of the fund, serious accountability cases exist in the administration of the fund. Citizens are not adequately involved to participate in the decision to disburse funds. This is also true of the MPs' share of the fund where consultations on identification of project and disbursement are more open to political rather than developmental considerations, and therefore liable to abuse.

While there are guidelines for utilization of the funds as set by the office of the administrator of the DACF, the arbitrary use of funds by some MPs, and the political influence exerted on the DAs' use of the district's allocations as intimated by assembly staff, suggest that either these rules are disregarded or are not effectively implemented. In fact the 'deduction from source' and 'earmarking' of allocations further opens DACF to abuse as how the funds are disbursed is not explicitly clear.

Accountability is therefore problematic. Some of the district assemblies lack capacity to manage the funds allocated to the districts. Studies show that some of the districts do not have proper documentation of the DACF, especially on some of the MPs' projects, suggesting that proper records are not kept on the use of the fund. There are no accountability procedures to monitor the use of resources once they have been accessed by MPs. The challenge is compounded by the conflict of interest of the MP who traditionally has an oversight responsibility, yet he/she is again a beneficiary of the fund at the same time.

The success of the fund?

The DACF constitutes a large source of resources for DAs and the benefits to the district and community has been considerable since the implementation of the programme. Through the DACF, infrastructure development of districts around the country has increased and in some communities perhaps under central government direct interventions would probably have been left out for a long time.

However, the implementation is confronted with problems associated with the allocations, disbursement and utilization of the fund. Several other concerns relate to delays and shortages in disbursements, misuse by MMDAs and some MPs, discrimination in the selection of projects (mainly on a partisan basis), and shoddy quality of projects executed as result of apparent flouting of procurement rules.

After two decades since the launch of the decentralization programme the huge rural–urban development gap is perhaps a better testimony of the need for reflection on national commitment to decentralization. While the rationale remains excellent, questions persist on whether the goals of decentralization are being realized.

The structural imbalances inherited from colonial policies are still not effectively addressed, as is evident in increasing rural deprivation versus relative urban improvement, despite twenty years of implementation of decentralization. There seems to be, on the contrary, centralization of development through control of both administration and resource use from central government. The excessive pressure on MPs to bring development to their districts instead of the executive machinery and the public service, is a statement to the effect that decentralization and the DACF are failing to deliver development to the citizenry. Against this background and challenges, perhaps such a constituency development fund as exists in other countries might be the answer, or a complementary source of funding for local development.

The constituency development fund in Ghana: recent developments

In his inaugural State of the Nation message in February 2009, President John Atta Mills announced the creation of constituency development fund. The President indicated that the Fund will replace the MPs' share of the District Assemblies Common Fund (DACF), which had become a source of tension between some district chief executives and MPs. His announcement elicited divergent views from members of the National Assembly of Ghana. While some MPs readily welcomed the announcement, others dismissed it as superfluous because, in their view, it will reinforce the idea that MPs are development agents. One MP lamented, 'already some constituents are in the habit of making incessant demands on MPs and the coming into being of this development fund will end up pitching the constituents against MPs'.

Honourable Appiah-Ofori, MP, an outspoken opposition MP and an anti-corruption crusader, pointed out that the Financial Administration Act 2003 does not allow those not authorized to sign cheques to draw from any public accounts. 'So if such an account is established it will in law form part of the accounts whose operation shall be under the District Finance Officer, so at the end of the day the obstacles which the MPs go through in accessing the development funds will still remain unchanged.'[2] Making a case for the CDF, Honourable Alfred Agbesi, MP for Ashiaman and from the ruling National Democratic Party (NDC), intimated that 'strictly, MPs are not development agents but society has imposed that duty on us the MPs'. He noted that even though district assemblies are given so many funds for development, less is said about it, 'but the little that comes to the MPs has always been a subject of disagreement'.[3]

It is posited that the creation of a parallel development fund outside the established structures also smacks of a vote of no confidence in the local governments and other constitutional organs charged with executing development programmes. Local governments under the 1992 Constitution of Ghana are charged with the preparation of comprehensive and integrated development plans incorporating plans of lower level councils for submission to the National Development Planning Commission. In this context, MPs with specific development plans to their constituencies should only ensure such plans are integrated into the local government's plans. The CDF is then sent as part of the central government conditional grant to the districts and not through the MPs.

The legislature, as an independent arm of government, should concentrate on its constitutional role of making good laws for peace, order and development and not engage in micromanagement of programmes.

In some countries such as Kenya, India and the Solomon Islands, the constituency development fund has an elaborate legal framework, premised on a policy that individual MPs have no direct access to the CDF funds. The MPs only participate with their constituencies to identify the projects to be funded by an amount set for the CDF during a particular financial year. Both the MPs and constituents participate in monitoring the implementation of the projects under the CDF. In Kenya, the CDF is governed by the Constituencies Development Act, 2003, and the Constituency Regulations Act, 2004. Both acts provide structures for the prudent governance and administration of the CDF. For a sustainable and effective operation of the constituency development fund in Ghana, the recommendations below will serve as critical pointers.

Key recommendations for CDF development in Ghana

First and foremost, there is the need to ensure a thorough review of the Local Government Act, which ushered in decentralization in Ghana. This is important because whatever form the future CDF in Ghana will take, it will be intricately linked to the decentralized structures of government. The Ministry of Local Government has been spearheading processes to reform the decentralization law. It is hoped that that process will take into account some of the lapses and challenges faced in the implementation of the DACF.

Apart from reform, another issue that is of paramount importance is one of voice and participation. The beneficiaries of the CDF in the constituencies should be involved in the selection and planning of the projects, so that they can participate in project implementation, monitoring and evaluation. The chosen projects should be submitted and explained by MPs to the local governments' planning committees, to ensure there is no duplication of the projects funded by the government. Whenever CDF money is disbursed, it should be publicized to create citizens' awareness and participation in the utilization and accountability of the fund. The CDF money should not be banked on the MPs' personal accounts or mixed with their other emoluments, but be banked on a separate account of local governments where the chief administrative officers should be part of the CDF management.

Other key recommendations include:

1   The clerk to Parliament should work closely with the chief administrative officers to ascertain the existence of a credible constituency committee to oversee the management of the CDF;
2   The CDF accountability and auditing procedures should be a function of the clerk to Parliament and the auditor-general, respectively;
3   The CDF should not simply be paid towards the end of any presidential/parliamentary term and/or impending elections to avoid a risk of exploiting the fund for personal political gain;
4   Finally, the media should be supported, trained and encouraged to focus their 'lenses' on accountability at the local level, particularly when the CDF comes into existence. This way they can help expose abuses.

Conclusion

Notwithstanding the optimism and pronouncements of advocates of the constituency development fund, it is posited that the CDF is unlikely to bring substantial developmental gains to citizens that cannot be realized through the DACF system if the system is streamlined and strengthened. And finally, the experiences of Kenya and Uganda and to a lesser extent Tanzania, should serve as cautionary tales to the members of Parliament and citizens of Ghana of what is likely to result if the CDF is introduced.

Notes

1   'Constituency' is interchangeable in this instance with 'district' to stress the electoral significance of such resources.
2   Interview with Hon. Appiah Ofori.
3   Interview with Hon. Agbesi.

15 Climate change
Establishing a continental parliamentary task force

David Ebong

A changing and challenging environment

Climate change is one of the largest challenges facing humanity this century. With direct linkages to development, climate change compounds the struggles already experienced by the world's poor. Developing countries are expected to be hit hardest by climate change and the impact on Africa is predicted to be more severe and exacerbate other ongoing pressures such as land degradation and water scarcity. Adaptation to these changes and better management of climate change risks are essential for many countries in Africa.

Parliaments have a crucial role to play in climate change adaptation and mitigation, providing relevant information, incentives, and economic environments conducive to adapting to changes and taking up new opportunities such as those from additional climate finance and climate-friendly technologies. It is within the primary functions of parliament – oversight, legislation, and representation – that we as members of Parliaments (MPs) must 'Act Now, Act Together and Act Differently'.

Increasing recognition of parliament's role in development as well as a rapidly changing climate led members of the Commonwealth Parliamentary Association (CPA) to form the Commonwealth Parliamentary Association Task Force on Climate Change (CPTFCC) in 2009. Anchored in the Task Force, a broader Community of Practice (CoP) has since developed, consisting of parliamentarians who are engaged on this issue and seek to address the impact of climate change in their respective countries. The CoP also provides a global platform for peer-to-peer knowledge exchange and a discussion on climate change issues between developed and developing countries outside the formal United Nations Framework Convention on Climate Change (UNFCCC) negotiations.

In an effort to determine how parliaments (both globally and within sub-Saharan Africa) can play a more constructive role in addressing the challenge of climate change, MPs and parliamentary staff from a cross section of sub-Saharan Africa countries[1] came together in May 2010 to form a study group on 'Parliament and Climate Change', hosted by Nigeria's National Assembly in Abuja, Nigeria.[2] The study group's primary objectives were:

1 To assess the knowledge and needs of parliaments in sub-Saharan Africa regarding climate change and its risks; responses to better manage these risks (adaptation); and efforts to reduce greenhouse gas emissions (mitigation);
2 To develop a body of knowledge focused on how parliaments can better contribute to the formulation, implementation and oversight of environmental policy in sub-Saharan Africa, especially as it relates to climate change; and
3 To provide guidance on the role MPs can play in facilitating implementation of climate change policies and strategies.

Recognizing that when it comes to parliamentary development, the true experts are the practitioners themselves – namely MPs – the best way to build the capacity of parliaments to engage in climate change issues is by convening a study group of MPs to facilitate knowledge-sharing. The study group discussions were able to capture rich examples of the successes and challenges faced by parliamentarians, champions of climate change reform in their own parliaments. It is clear that we as MPs want to understand how to provide leadership in terms of climate change policies, legal frameworks, and sectors within the context of budgetary and infrastructure constraints. This chapter illustrates the ideas study group members brought forward as they were addressed: through the main functions of parliament.

A case study on Uganda's Parliamentary Forum on Climate Change (PFCC) will be used throughout the chapter to demonstrate the intersections of climate change and Parliament's primary functions. Formed in 2008, the Forum – the first in Africa – is a mechanism through which Uganda can strengthen linkages between the parliament, executive, and civil society on climate change and related challenges through representation, legislation and oversight. Born out of the Ugandan Parliamentary Committee on Natural Resources, the forum serves as a conduit to prompt action from key stakeholders. The bipartisan independent forum consists of over 200 MPs as well as development practitioners, the private sector, and civil society organizations.

According to the forum's website, the members resolve to act upon three priority areas, namely 'streamlining climate change issues into the national budget, creating a communications strategy, [and] implementing a training program for all members';[3] the last priority aspires to broaden the reach of information acquired in the trainings as forum members relay knowledge back to their constituencies. The forum is headed by an executive committee and funded by the British Embassy to Uganda, the Association of European Parliamentarians for Africa (AWEPA), and the Department for International Development (DfID). The forum is supported by a program coordinator as well as a financial officer in its secretariat. These administrators support the forum by facilitating inter-agency coordination, consulting with relevant parliamentary committees and forging partnerships within, *inter alia*, the executive, local governments, and media.

Representation and climate change

The Study Group determined that the relationship between climate change and parliament's representative function is twofold: (i) to reflect citizens' best interests in managing climate change adaptation and mitigation through oversight and legislation; and (ii) to convey to constituents the grave dangers faced by a warming planet as well as ways they can adapt to and reduce carbon emissions.

A fundamental challenge MPs face both within parliament and externally in their constituencies is the lack of an accessible definition of climate change and a common understanding of the issues related to climate change, including adaptation, mitigation, existing and potential climate-finance mechanisms, and the relationship with development. The causal relationship between development and climate change is multifaceted and requires an understanding and, potentially, a change in mindset of both citizens and MPs; for example, it is important to recognize that changes in frequency and intensity of floods and droughts affects food production and thus food security, which in turn can affect income, trade, and the health of farmers and their families.

Building awareness of climate change, its anthropogenic causes and dangerous impacts on society, as well as its relationship to the environment and economy, is central to providing an incentive for constituents to act. In fact, the mandate of Uganda's Forum is 'To promote awareness and action about the effects of climate change [and] [t]o ensure society-wide resilience against climate change through targeted capacity building.' Leaders in the community, parliament, and the executive should understand the relationship between climate change and development, acknowledging the cross-cutting nature of climate change in creating obstacles for achieving the Millennium Development Goals. Ultimately, without these key stakeholders, change will not occur.

Engagement with civil society is a key means by which to communicate with constituents; maximizing outreach opportunities through civil society channels also serves as a resource to parliament when its own resources are limited. However, it is important to distinguish between advocacy groups and beneficiary organizations. The role of some civil society organizations (CSOs) is not in direct programme delivery even though their mandate may appear so; parliamentarians have found it necessary to be conscious of the different roles CSOs can play in the policy and oversight process.

The forum provides a notable example of how parliament can engage with civil society. It is similar to a parliamentary caucus, yet encourages participation by civil society through dialogue meetings, small working groups with three to four MPs who take on specific issues and report back to civil society. Dialogue meetings provide an opportunity for members and key stakeholders to discuss and determine initiatives that correspond to the priorities of the forum. Civil society and MPs are able to ask critical questions of each other and ultimately MPs prioritize the issues they will take forward and determine a time frame for the forum members to reconvene and evaluate progress made. Moreover, civil society can take on leadership positions within the forum; a civil society representative chairs the forum's group on Reducing Emissions from Deforestation and Forest Degradation.

This operational structure facilitates a free flow of information between Uganda's government, Parliament, and civil society. Additional ways Uganda's MPs benefit from civil society include learning how CSOs sustain strong climate change practices, meeting with CSOs to receive insight on policy briefs highlighting policy gaps, and collaborating on community outdoor broadcasts in which CSOs find hotspots to conduct and document public dialogues. Many CSOs may have a larger capacity to document discussions than do MPs, which creates an impetus for Parliament to create opportunities for civil society to be more active in engaging various parliaments. Much of the feedback received from CSOs is issue-based and provides substantive input that can be used when performing Parliament's legislative and oversight functions. However, Uganda's Parliament, in always exploring new ways of sharing knowledge, has instigated engagement with the East African Community and bilateral aid agencies to share tools and build strong networking and institutional linkages.

Similarly, the media provides an opportunity to enhance communication with constituents. The study group linked Parliament's representative function with interaction and partnership with the media and public hearings in committees or forums to disseminate information on climate change. Public hearings promote two-way communication between legislators and the community, whilst encouraging the media to report on deliberations. Moreover, bolstering the work of a parliamentary press corps through improved access, training and resources provides an entry point for MPs to engage with the press corps, simultaneously building the corps' knowledge base of climate change whilst understanding the freedoms and limitations of Parliament.

Legislation and climate change

Parliament's representative function is a precursor to legislative action as it provides a solid base by which to coordinate and pass policies. The study group shared strategies and mechanisms employed in their respective countries to organize themselves internally on climate change issues, focusing to a large extent on how to better use parliamentary committees to ensure robust climate-change-related legislation is passed. Additionally, participants discussed climate change policy formulation and regulation, with some progress being made, but to various degrees. Members also took the opportunity to share the legislative and structural experiences of their parliaments.

Study group members agreed that their respective parliaments should collaborate with the executive to pass legislation so as to domesticate international climate change obligations. Some protocols do require binding agreements by parliaments, yet most often MPs are excluded from the decision-making process, unaware of international commitments made by the executive. In Botswana, for example, particularly since COP 15,[4] climate change issues remain in the ministerial domain as international treaties and conventions are ratified by the executive. For example, although Botswana's executive consults with Parliament at the point of treaty domestication, major challenges manifest when the executive takes an extensive amount of time to internally discuss the international agreements and subsequently asks Parliament to review the agreements within a short time frame.

In Uganda, the forum's efforts towards regional coalition building also aim to contribute to the preparation for international climate change negotiations. It is in this context that the forum has anchored itself as a promoter of an African Parliamentary Network on Climate Change with the African Union. This Network intends to serve as an arena for discussions on international climate change negotiations so as to provide a more united African front at upcoming UNFCCC negotiations. In this vein, and as a follow-up to the study group in Abuja, the Uganda Forum was able to convene 'The Regional Parliamentary Symposium in Uganda: Strategic Planning to Address Climate Change', an initial meeting in August 2010 between MPs from Uganda, the East Africa Legislative Assembly and the South Africa Development Cooperation region.

In bringing together multiple stakeholders, the forum acts as an advocacy group in Parliament, lobbying for climate change policies, policy reforms, and policy harmonization. Passing and regulating (and in some cases introducing)legislation is a primary function of Parliament; ensuring climate change is not overlooked and that policies adequately address climate change is a significant task which the forum seeks to support. Botswana's Parliament faces hurdles in introducing and passing climate change related bills as MPs meet resistance when bringing a private bill to Parliament.[5] Uganda has a number of climate change policies in place, but struggles with the government's failure to implement and enforce them; the judiciary has not come onboard and help is needed to build their capacity to understand and enforce climate-change-related laws.

Conversely, Ghana has succeeded in passing climate-change-related legislation. Ghana developed a draft national policy on climate change which provides for the inclusion of strategic environmental assessments (SEAs), allowing legislators to take climate change into account when reviewing the policies and programmes associated with private- and public-sector projects.[6]

Oversight and climate change

Frameworks for oversight

Study group discussions on the legislative and representative roles of parliament in climate change served as an impetus for delving into budget and oversight concerns. Participants concluded parliaments should be able to oversee the implementation of government policies aimed at climate-resilient and low-carbon development, influencing budgeting processes and providing oversight for line-items related to climate change in the budget. The current capacity of African parliaments to engage in the budget process is limited, but the ability of MPs sitting on lead climate change committees to influence budgeting outcomes or provide implementation oversight is even more challenging. MPs' roles and functions need to be strengthened in order to make headway in developing systems that result in representative, accountable and sustainable development and climate change strategies.

Committees in each country do not have the same structures or priorities; some countries have climate change committees and others have committees which take the responsibility of climate change affairs under their domain. The study group discussed three basic models parliaments appear to have adopted on committee structure and oversight functions, representing comprehensive and targeted approaches. Participants agreed further examination of these and other models is needed.

In Figure 15.1, Model 1 illustrates a lead oversight committee which provides direct oversight for an intergovernmental agency or central ministry. In some circumstances, the committee has power to refer oversight roles to subcommittees or other standing committees. The Gambia most resembles Model 1 as it has a number of different committees which handle climate change concerns including the Committee on Environment and Sustainable Development and the Monitoring and Evaluation Committee, which engages in climate change issues as it oversees the work of other committees. Under the executive, climate change concerns are handled and implemented by the Ministry of Forestry and the Environment. Like the Gambia, Zambia's oversight framework most closely resembles Model 1; climate change issues are directed to the Committee on Energy, Environment, and Tourism which is responsible for overseeing the Ministry of Tourism,

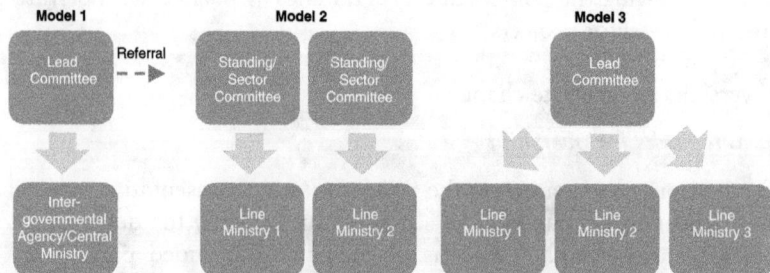

Figure 15.1 Climate change committee structure and oversight function models

Environment, and Natural Resources as well as the Ministry of Energy and Water Development.

Model 2 represents the absence of a specific oversight committee but demonstrates a case where a number of committees oversee line ministries. The model also allows for shared or overlapping membership to allow common coordination. Nigeria's National Assembly has been very proactive in seeking to pass legislative and regulatory reform to address climate change challenges, and houses many committees which address climate change. Each committee is independent of the other; however, if there are common issues shared by committees, members meet to resolve them. Nigeria's government also has a number of ministries which address climate change (as well as an Inter-Ministerial Committee on Climate Change); as such, this multi-sectoral approach most resembles Model 2, with arrows not only pointing vertically but horizontally.

Model 3 presents a lead committee that has the responsibility of overseeing the implementation of climate change policy across all line ministries. Senegal's Parliament has an Environment and Agriculture Committee consisting of 20 MPs who work on all rural activities. At the government level there are various ministers for agriculture, environment, and other issues concerning climate change, corresponding to Model 3.

Uganda's forum engages with the executive as a key stakeholder. As previously mentioned, the forum operates through small dialogue meetings focusing on particular issues. In some cases, issues require responses from respective ministries; MPs use informal questions to line ministries (working through clerks of committees) and request that they make a formal written reply which is presented to committees and subsequently recounted to civil society for their feedback and input. The executive must respond to the committees' request, as under the Ugandan Constitution they have the power of high court. Moreover, this process has facilitated a good working relationship between government and civil society, providing an example of how MPs can bridge the gap between CSOs and government in order to help promote more responsive policies

Ultimately, the executive must also take the initiative to engage Parliament, however. The Government of Uganda's Ministry of Water and Environment, housed in the Department of Meteorology, formed a Climate Change Unit (CCU) in 2009. Beyond having been designated to spearhead the Ugandan government in climate change reform and international negotiations, the CCU – in its list of responsibilities – is required to informally report to the forum; this type of feedback mechanism is undeniably valuable in the forum's work as a partner in engaging Uganda in the climate change agenda.

The study group concluded that it is difficult for a committee to oversee climate change issues unless it has the proper governance framework. Given the need to reduce the impacts of climate change and move towards low carbon development which can provide multiple benefits to society, the group reinforced that good governance was essential in achieving positive sustainable development and climate change outcomes.

Budget oversight

When a proper governance framework is in place, parliament's financial oversight powers are pivotal to ensure climate change reforms are being implemented. There are also various tools parliaments can employ in their efforts to scrutinize budgets. For example, most countries in Africa have national plans or Poverty Reduction Strategy frameworks for national plans. Parliament can examine whether the government's budget reflects policy the priorities of the plan. A simple analysis will show whether enough is allocated to necessary agencies within ministries. When parliament receives the budget and it is evident priorities do not reflect policy intentions, parliament may be able to ask for changes; even in systems where allocation increases aren't possible, MPs can look for redistribution opportunities. It is easier to scrutinize budget implementation in the *ex-post* phase if parliament has overseen appropriation bills in the *ex-ante* phase.

Scrutiny is possible particularly in activity-based budgeting countries: for each department there are stated objectives, activities to meet those objectives, and resources required. Often this oversight will demonstrate budgets that mostly cover meetings, office supplies, accommodations and consultants. Issues of policy and programme implementation and outreach are seldom detailed. As indicated, collaboration with civil society may yield resources outside of the government such as provision of field sites which can fulfil parliamentary needs. MPs should review the revenue side of budgets to identify sources of funding.

When compiling an implementation report *ex-post*, assessment is crucial. In many systems the directive is to give a report on a new budget once implementation is achieved. Governments will provide audit reports after the accounting period but are not clear about actual resource use. It is up to MPs to ask the right questions and invoke the right sanctions. For example, a new act in Kenya makes the provision to withhold new allocations unless committees receive appropriate financial reports; such laws can be proposed in parliaments.

The power of the purse is the greatest power of parliament, a power that can shape a climate-change-friendly budget. As some study group countries[7] have been involved in developing National Adaptation Programmes of Action (NAPAs), NAPAs can be used as a strategy to deal with climate change issues and act as a blueprint for miti-gation as well as adaptation strategies. NAPAs can be used by par-liaments looking at priorities that are often developed by ministries of the environment, ensuring the executive is following through on its plans. However it should be noted NAPAs can also provide co-ordination but are funded by specific isolated funds which are not overseen by parliament.

Budget and policy implementation is usually done by a key com-mittee in parliament (often a public accounts committee or PAC in anglophone countries and a finance committee in francophone sys-tems). Supreme audit institutions (SAIs) are chief tools for financial auditing, which can contribute to the monitoring, reporting and verifi-cation (MFV) efforts currently being discussed in the UNFCCC party negotiations. The international community is moving towards climate-change-based auditing which is similar to performance-based auditing. In fact, the International Organization for Supreme Audit Institutions (INTOSAI) is working to create standards to conduct comprehensive climate change audits.

Not all parliamentarians have the capacity to influence the budget. In Benin, even if Parliament votes against the proposed budget, it can still be passed by the executive. Tanzanian MPs also do not have a final say on the budget, although it must still go the House for review and every MP has a chance to make comments. The time frame for reviewing the budget has proven challenging, but is in the pro-cess of shifting to a longer time period with multiple consultation opportunities.

Indeed oversight is a priority for Uganda's forum, particularly oversight of government budgets. Members of the forum seek to sup-port Parliament in ensuring budgets are responsive to climate change and promote climate change adaptation and mitigation initiatives. Partnering with civil society organizations and the media to help in these efforts serves as an important asset to Parliament, which often struggles with limited human and financial resources. In Uganda the forum has a strategic plan to engage the media and encourage it to do investigative journalism on accountability through the lens of climate change.

In summary, the study group's oversight discussions highlighted how essential it is to find windows for MPs to be a part of the budgetary process. Committee and intergovernmental structures, and their lines of accountability, are crucial to exercising parliament's capacity to oversee government climate change policies and programme implementation. As noted previously, using civil society as a resource is valuable, whether it be to conduct carbon audits or receive feedback on budget reports.

Recommendations

The study group concluded their discussions by developing a body of recommendations.[8] By parliamentarians and for parliamentarians, the recommendations offer guidance for MPs to play a more constructive role in addressing the challenge of climate change as well as spurring awareness, debate, and further research. They are structural along the main functions of parliament, namely representative (including engaging with civil society), legislative, and oversight.

Conclusion

This chapter synthesized knowledge shared during the study group, including a number of examples of the successes and challenges faced by parliamentarians who have been champions of climate change reform in their own parliaments. In particular, the case study of Uganda's Parliamentary Forum on Climate Change highlighted several ways parliament can lead a country in effective climate change legislation, facilitate multi-stakeholder dialogues and ensure climate-change-related policies and finances are being applied as intended. The example of the forum provided study group members with ideas on how parliaments can better contribute to the formulation, implementation and oversight of environmental policy in sub-Saharan Africa, especially as it relates to climate change.

Ultimately, the study group agreed that parliamentarians in Africa need to have a change in attitude with respect to climate change as it is a relatively new and complex issue. Leaders need to acknowledge that they (i) have a responsibility to understand an issue as thoroughly as possible and be open to listening to new information, providing the best possible solutions; and (ii) have a great deal of power – the more MPs become involved in an issue, the more the executive is willing to take action. Encouraging MPs to take action on a particular issue is a challenge, considering each MP starts from the perspective of what is in his/her own interest; however, the potential to build the capacity for interest and leadership in the arena of climate change is high. The cross-cutting nature of climate change allows many MPs to engage on this agenda, particularly as it relates to sustainable development.

Notes

1 Benin, Botswana, the Gambia, Ghana, Nigeria, Senegal, Tanzania, Uganda, and Zambia.
2 The study group was convened by the Commonwealth Parliamentary Association (CPA) and the World Bank Institute (WBI), in partnership with the Parliamentary Centre and the Association of European Parliamentarians in Africa (AWEPA), and with support from the Commonwealth Secretariat.
3 http://www.parliament.go.ug/index.php?option=com_content&task=view&id=410&Itemid=138.
4 http://unfccc.int/meetings/cop_15/items/5257.php.
5 Since the study group, Botswana has formed a Standing Committee on Climate Change and climate change has been selected as a key security concern for Botswana.
6 For more on SEAs and climate change, read the United Kingdom Government's 'Strategic Environmental Assessment and climate change: Guidance for practitioners' accessible at: http://www.environment-agency.gov.uk/static/documents/Research/seaccjune07_1797458.pdf.
7 Benin, the Gambia, Tanzania, and Uganda.
8 http://www.cpahq.org/cpahq/cpadocs/CC%20Study%20Group%20Recommendations.pdf.

16 Strengthening public accounts committees through regional networks across Africa

John M. Cheyo

Public Accounts Committees (PACs) oversee the spending of government ministries and institutions. In South Africa, the Association of PACs (APAC) is an association for South African PACs, and links these provincial and national committees together to pursue common goals and objectives. It creates a platform for the sharing of experiences between all institutions that are accountable to the legislative authorities of South Africa. APAC gets together each year, and invites representatives from other African PACs to its meetings.

Inspired by the success of APAC, it was at the APAC annual meeting in 2002 when representatives of national PACs within the Southern African Development Community resolved to form the Southern African Development Community Organisation of Public Accounts Committees (SADCOPAC). SADCOPAC is an autonomous and independent association of PACs from SADC states, established to strengthen public accounts committees. Its mission is to promote accountability, good governance and transparency by fostering the exchange of ideas, knowledge and experiences between PACs and to act as a recognized voice of PACs within the SADC community. The organization's members are Botswana, Lesotho, Malawi, Mauritius, Mozambique, Namibia, Seychelles, South Africa, Swaziland, Tanzania and Zambia.

SADCOPAC's constitution, mission, and objectives

The Tanzanian Auditor-General at that time took the lead by offering to host SADCOPAC's first meeting in Tanzania and to house the SADCOPAC Secretariat in his office, the National Audit Office, where the Secretariat still remains today. The organization was officially launched in October 2003 in Johannesburg, South Africa. Eight months after the launch the first annual SADCOPAC conference and annual general meeting were held in Tanzania in June 2004. At this meeting the executive committee was ratified, and a constitution was adopted.

The constitution sets out the objectives of SADCOPAC, as well as guidelines for its operations. According to the constitution, SADCOPAC shall strive to distinguish itself as an organization empowering the representatives of each member state to effectively carry out their functions as oversight committees over public sector finances. It will continuously facilitate the efficiency of spending by promoting sound management practices, based on transparent and accountable governance.

SADCOPAC has eight specific objectives:

1   Work with governments and other relevant players on sound and accountable governance;
2   Build capacity and expertise among members to effectively carry out their oversight functions and duties;
3   Conduct research and share best practices;
4   Improve the effectiveness of PACs within the SADC region;
5   Harmonize and standardize the work of PACs in the SADC region;
6   Communicate and build relationships with individuals and organizations with relevant expertise;
7   Empower members to disseminate information on the work and activities of PACs among the executive, other members of parliament, the media and the general public;
8   Liaise with the Southern African Development Community Organization of Supreme Audit Institutions (SADCOSAI).

The annual meeting

The annual meeting is SADCOPAC's most important event. Every year, the conference is hosted by the country that has chairmanship of SADCOPAC, which is a different member country each year. After the first meeting in Tanzania, the annual event has been held in Namibia, Mozambique, Malawi and most recently Zambia. The annual meetings serve as a platform for dialogue and discussion and are designed to facilitate the sharing of information and experiences among SADC's PACs. The agenda of the meeting is very much member-driven and structured around a theme that relates to the PACs' mandate of overseeing government expenditures, like enhancing the effectiveness of PACs, value-for-money audits, and integrated financial management systems. Experts in the field are invited to present, and the delegates are given the opportunity to question the speakers after each presentation. Networking among PACs is a valuable way of strengthening public accountability and building oversight capacity of legislators. Learning how PACs in other jurisdictions have tackled problems is a central aspect of exchanging ideas and I think the process has shown us how effective peer review is as a learning method – PACs working in comparable environments understand your struggles very well.

SADCOPAC has been applauded for including different participants from both the legislature and the executive in the conferences. SADCOPAC also works in close collaboration with supreme audit institutions such as the offices of the auditor-generals (AGs). The relation between PACs and AGs is cardinal to the prudent utilization of public resources. Supreme audit institutions are affiliated to SADCOPAC and participate in its activities. SADCOPAC brings members of parliament and auditors-general from East and West Africa to the conference as well[1].

After each conference, delegates are requested to develop resolutions on how to enhance the effectiveness of PACs in public financial management and accountability, based on the presentations and topics discussed at the meeting. In their own country, the resolutions are used as proof and evidence to convince Parliament of what needs to be done to improve PAC performance.

In the months after the meeting, all member states must then submit a written progress report on progress on the implementation of the resolutions, which is to be submitted to the SADCOPAC secretariat. If a country is not making (sufficient) progress there are no sanctions, but the SADCOPAC meetings create a form of accountability among members, so that they feel pressure to deliver on the resolutions in order to avoid uncomfortable situations when facing their peers.

An effective public accounts committee

PACs face serious challenges in effectively performing their oversight function in many African countries. Some of these challenges are:

- Dealing with outdated audit reports;
- Accounting officers that do not respond to queries from the PAC;
- A lack of understanding of the financial regulations by the PAC members;
- The executive not implementing the recommendations of the PAC;

- A misperception that oversight is the responsibility of the opposition;
- Members showing allegiance to political parties rather than fulfilling the responsibility of a PAC.

At the annual meetings it was decided that a minimum standardization of accounting practices, accounting systems and PAC operating procedures was necessary. One of the first questions that came up during the meeting was *'Which elements make for an effective PAC?'* We know from experience and research that there are several elements to an effective PAC. For instance, the PAC should be guided by respected, moral, and social leadership; the chair should be from an opposition party; ministers should not serve on the PAC; there should be a clear statement of mandate, power, and reporting practices; the PAC's size should be about 10 members; there should be well-functioning research and analytical infrastructure in place; the PAC should be served by an independent AG; the PAC should commit to the principles of transparency and accountability; the term of the PAC should be equal to the term of the legislature.

Unfortunately, most PACs in SADC countries lack the elements required for an effective committee, although the country experiences indicate varying degrees of challenges. In order to strengthen PACs' effectiveness, the following resolutions were adopted:

1 PACs must acquire the status of standing committee with a term of office that would foster continuity and institutional memory;
2 PAC hearings should be open to the public as far as possible;
3 PACs must ensure that there is an effective mechanism within parliament to follow up and monitor responses from government in relation to PAC resolutions;
4 PACs must strive to have their own budgets.

In the case of Botswana, there used to be a new PAC with each session of parliament, so that MPs could only serve on the PAC for a 12-month period. SADCOPAC's resolutions recommended that MPs serving on a PAC should do so for a full legislative period. Thanks to the resolutions, the tenure of PAC membership in Botswana increased to two and a half years, while the Chair's tenure is being extended to four to five years, to ensure continuity.

As a Chairman I have been trying hard to improve the efficiency and influence of the PAC in Tanzania. For instance, it is now mandatory for the government to respond to the PAC report and its recommendations. The new standing orders that were adopted in 2008 ensure that the PAC, as a select committee, can propose a bill in the House. An office of legal advisor to parliament is there to assist the committee in legislative drafting. In 2007, for the first time in history, the PAC report was made public after pressure on the government to release it. Other than that, the AG is now independent, and has to report directly to Parliament instead of to the executive. Moreover, the budget of the AG and the comptroller must be approved by Parliament, and after approval the Ministry of Finance cannot change the allocated amount.

Other best practices transferred

There are several other best practices or methods that have been discussed by our peers at our meetings.

- Parliaments in the region have made considerable progress towards calling their executives to account for the utilization of public resources, but they face several hurdles such as the lack of legal frameworks and poor coordination with law-enforcement agencies on how to better carry out oversight. At our 2009 conference in Zambia, we learned that in Uganda the PAC works closely together with national law-enforcement agencies like the police, in order to fight against corruption. This method has been very successful in Uganda, and SADCOPAC is now exploring the possibilities for PACs within the SADC region to work together with the police and/or national anti-corruption agencies in order to make sure that public officials suspected of having misused public moneys are prosecuted.
- Related to the previous point, SADCOPAC is trying to persuade governments to enact laws to implement the recommendations of PACs. This way, public officials who have misused public funds will be more easily punished, which would make auditing of public accounts a more meaningful task. Previously, there was no law to compel national governments in SADC to act on resolutions of PACs, but SADCOPAC urges governments to enact laws to implement the recommendations against erring officers. SADOPAC has committed itself to punish those who misuse public funds.
- At our last annual meeting I learned that it might prove useful for PACs to interview public officials in front of the camera and then air the dialogue on national TV. At first I was sceptical and I hesitated, but the SADCOPAC presentation convinced me to

try it out. We decided to interview two people: a regional administrator who was responsible for the payment of salary to a person
that should have already retired, and the Clerk of the House, who
we asked for an explanation about the budget that was set aside to
build or restore his office, but that had for some reason increased
by 300 per cent. It turned out to be a great success, as we got many
reactions from people all over the country. I find it a good way of
creating accountability because people can really see their public
officials talking. We are definitely going to be using this method of
oversight more often in the future.

- SADCOPAC members decided to lobby their respective parliaments to strengthen their capacities and that of the AGs to enable auditing and review of state-owned enterprises. Some SADC
member states do not yet have legislation in place that allows for
this auditing.

- SADCOPAC wants to comply with the international trend to
enhance the independence of supreme audit institutions. Currently
in many SADC countries it seems as if the AG is the internal auditor of the government, while it should be operating as an independent external auditor of the state. SADCOPAC is convincing
its members that it is crucial for PACs to have a good working
relationship with the AG, as the PAC depends on the AG for its
work. Other than that, SADCOPAC is pushing its member countries to make sure legislation is in place that makes the AG report
directly to parliament.

Struggles

SADCOPACs two main struggles are a lack of capacity of PAC members, and a lack of finance for activities. Let me illustrate this with an
example.

The focus of PACs has shifted away from a review of whether the
government is spending funds correctly to performance audits or so-
called value-for-money audits. Doing a performance audit means that
the output delivered will be reviewed against costs and quality, really
getting to the bottom of *how* and *on what* the money has been spent.
It turns out that the reality on the ground is often different to what it
looks like on paper. Unfortunately, so far there has been little progress
on implementing performance auditing in member states. There are
two reasons for this.

First, neither PACs nor AGs have the necessary skills available to
undertake such audits. Indeed, it is very difficult to find experienced

staff with a financial background even for regular audits. The parliamentary staff supporting PACs are sometimes not permanent and are moved around a lot to help out other committees. Furthermore, the MPs that serve on PACs are typically not elected because of their knowledge of accounting and whether or not they know how to read a financial statement. As a result, there is a need to train and build the capacity of both the Committee's members and staff to carry out assigned tasks.

The limitations on resources bring me to the second reason. Both PACs and AGs face constraint by the lack of funds available to carry out performance audits. One way of doing a performance audit is to go and check projects that the money has been spent on. This can have instant benefits. For example, with the Tanzanian PAC I recently visited a water dam project that meant to provide water to communities. The project had been going for 32 years and its costs were increasing dramatically. When we got there to check its progress we found that there still was no water available to the communities. Since the PAC came to take a look, activities have accelerated and the people in the area now have access to water. Travelling to these areas is costly, and it is unlikely SADCOPAC member states are able to fund field visits for PAC members on a regular basis. We have to sit together and find ways of how to make value-for-money audits operable in an environment where money, equipment and human resources are not readily available. Performance auditing is crucial, but we also have to train ourselves and the AG on how to conduct these types of audit.

The same is true for other issues than performance audits. Integrated financial management systems (IFMS), for instance, have been an interesting topic at our annual conferences. The problem is that PACs face resource constraints in the form of lack of skilled staff, lack of equipment, and inadequate financing to adopt IFMS.

Future prospects

SADCOPAC produces strategic plans to effectively monitor and scrutinize the utilization of public funds. In its most recent strategic framework, which covers the years 2009 to 2012, SADCOPAC prioritized its activities and direction strategically. For the upcoming years SADCOPAC will focus on capacity-building for staff, research the financial-management legislation across SADC countries, create benchmarks for best practices, and try to harmonize and formalize financial-management systems. We have also decided to devote time to procurement issues at our annual conference, as the embezzlement of public funds through dubious contracts can accrue very large amounts of money. A country's development goes hand in hand with good contracts which save public funds from misuse.

The biggest challenge by far is to obtain adequate funds and develop the infrastructure that would support the PACs' work. Due to small budgets set aside for PACs within member states, activities cannot be carried out only by national parliament's contributions. SADCOPAC needs a helping hand. To find sufficient funds to implement its activities and continue to support PACs, SADCOPAC has developed a fundraising campaign. The money is meant for continuous training of PAC members and clerks of parliament that support PACs. The SADCOPAC Secretariat advises member countries to be very active in the development of SADCOPAC programs and their implementation as this will be a powerful way of persuading donors, including national parliaments, to fund our activities. In order to improve transparency and accountability among ourselves and towards donors, SADCOPAC wants to improve its communication and has initiated an active website and regularly produces a newsletter.

The seeds of this organization have taken root and if progress made so far continues into the future, SADCOPAC will grow into a self-sustaining and credible regional body. I am convinced that accountability is only enforceable if there are processes in place that are transparent, and if clear rules and regulations for national financial management are set. We are arming ourselves with the duty the public expects from us.

Note

1   Indeed, PACs in both regions have followed SADCOPAC's approach and founded their own regional associations – the East African Association of PACs (EAAPAC) and the West African Association of PACs (WAAPAC).

17 The role of parliamentarians in the governance of petroleum resources

AbdulKarim Mohammed

General concepts

As is the case with all extractive resources which are finite, the governance of petroleum requires prudent and effective policies, legislations and institutions to ensure lasting benefits to all citizens of a nation both today and for generations yet unborn. To achieve this, resource-rich nations need to establish a governance framework that allows efficient resource management and regulation as well as a predictable fiscal regime. The process, from discovery of the natural resource and how is transformed to benefits for citizens, is summarised in the illustration below (Figure 17.1).

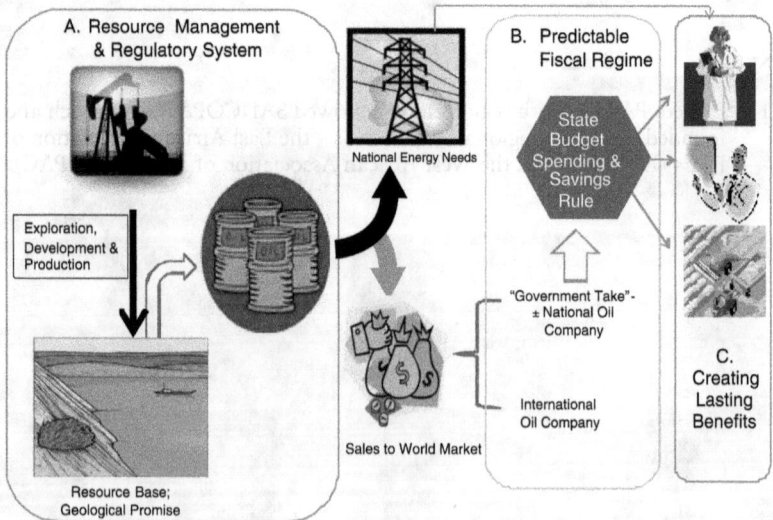

Figure 17.1 Petroleum sector governance framework

From the illustration, it is observed that the mere discovery of petroleum resource or establishing the so-called geological promise is not sufficient to derive the potential benefits to a nation. Rather, a good governance framework that is enabling for resource exploration, development and production to either satisfy local energy needs or for foreign exchange must be of prime interest to the nation.

In such an intricate and sensitive sector of strategic interest for nations, parliamentarians have a principal role to play around the trilogy of their representative, legislative and oversight mandates across the petroleum value chain (Figure 17.2) – i.e. the decision to extract the resources; negotiation and award of licenses and contracts; development programmes/projects thereof.

The value chain is the foundation for the governance of extractives as it provides a comprehensive coverage of all the stages involved in resource management. It depicts how non-renewable resources in the ground can be transformed into improved public welfare and the chain is only as strong as its weakest link because each of the links in the chain represents an opportunity seized or squandered.

Good petroleum governance requires a long-term vision for the role of the oil and gas sector in national development, which has to be realistic and be founded on a sound understanding of the resource base.

As representatives of the people, members of parliament (MPs) are well placed to ensure that government policy goals for the sector are clear and reflect the hopes and aspirations of citizens. Such a policy must be borne out of a broad national development agenda that spells out development targets such as economic growth, employment for nationals, value creation in the country, local participation, induced expenditure in the local economy, enhanced human/enterprising capacity, as well as technology transfer, among other things. The broad framework should also address the nature of state participation and benefits to host communities where petroleum activities are carried out in relation to the provision of alternative livelihood schemes in places where traditional economic activities are interfered with and environmental concerns adequately addressed. The realisation of policy objectives demands that effective institutions backed by the necessary pieces of legislation are well established.

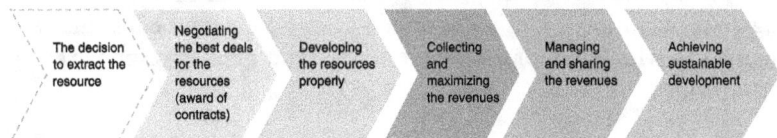

| The decision to extract the resource | Negotiating the best deals for the resources (award of contracts) | Developing the resources properly | Collecting and maximizing the revenues | Managing and sharing the revenues | Achieving sustainable development |

Figure 17.2 The extractives value chain

On the legislative front, parliament is the single most important institution that can determine whether the final legal framework for the governance of petroleum is adequate or not. With a mandate as the law-making body, parliament has the responsibility of ensuring that the laws in place are sufficiently enabling to allow for policy objectives to be achieved; that laws are enacted into effective regulations; that individual license agreements are enforceable and consistent with policy and regulations; and that the systems and institutions are in place to ensure compliance with health, safety and environment standards and to achieve policy objectives. In relation to a finite resource that suffers one of the worst forms of price volatility, fiscal prudence for securing a stable economy and savings for future generations anchored in law is the *sine qua non* for good resource governance that only parliament can guarantee. The legislature occupies a unique position to ensure that transparent and accountable decision-making and conflict-resolution mechanisms are in place. To achieve all the above will need a lot of bipartisanship and consensus building. A successful petroleum industry will require not just good sector-specific laws but rather the entire legal framework must be adequately enabling.

A follow-up to the establishment of a robust legal and institutional framework is effective oversight. Effective parliamentary oversight in democratic societies is the prime mover to ensuring that all parties charged with responsibilities live up to expectations. Good laws and institutions are not an end in themselves but rather a means to an end. Having passed good laws to help in governing the petroleum sector, it is the duty of parliament to undertake continuous monitoring with the view of ensuring that there is full compliance. As the saying goes, 'In God we trust, all others we monitor.' Through the mechanisms/processes such as the Extractive Industries Transparency Initiative (EITI) and the Public Accounts Committee, parliaments can ensure greater transparency and accountability beyond revenue to include contracts transparency and performance audit. All actors must be made to understand that they will be held to account for their stewardship and parliaments are required to lead the way on this. Good parliamentary leadership will require self-assessment of the performance of parliament itself in terms of the kind of laws and agreements ratified. This will provide MPs, beside their constitutional mandate, with the moral courage to demand greater responsiveness from all.

Parliamentary Functions across the petroleum value chain

Award of contracts is the first substantive engagement of parliament in petroleum governance. Ideally, award of contracts should emanate from government policy on resource management and licensing of resource rights. At this stage a cost–benefit analysis should made to establish whether a nation is not better off with its oil left underground than exploited.

In Ghana, Parliament is the body vested with the authority to ratify agreements/contracts, after all the boardroom negotiations. The key issue that should be of primary concern to MPs at the stage of awarding contracts is who can explore and exploit the resources and how are such rights allocated? Experiences across the globe indicate that open access to title through a competitive bid process provides the host nation a better opportunity to assess prospective companies with diverse experiences and capabilities and offers of a better deal. This demands that parliamentarians, especially members of the relevant committees with direct responsibility for the petroleum sector, should have very good understanding of what such agreements or contracts entail. Typically, before the ratification of an agreement on the floor of Parliament, the committee-level assessment will fall in the domain of the Joint Committee of Mines and Energy and Finance. A key consideration for optimal exploitation of resources is the technical capability of the company. This will require that due diligence is carried out to verify any claim of competence on the part of the company. Also of great importance are the fiscal and non-fiscal benefits as these are what accrue to the nation in both monetary and non-monetary terms. Of particular importance is the issue of stabilisation clause(s) that tends to preclude companies from the variation of the fiscal terms. Though the host nation is encouraged to provide a stable and predictable fiscal environment as a tool to incentivize investors, this should not be at the disadvantage of the nation. Provisions should be made for the host nation to benefit from all possible benefits, including windfalls. Additionally, safeguards against negative health, safety, environmental and social impacts are to be considered and this will require an input from the Committee on Environment. Often forgotten is the issue of abandonment after the productive years of the oil fields. In assessing agreements, MPs should address themselves to ensure that adequate provision is made to cater for removal of installations either on the seabed or onshore as far as is practicable. It is also at this stage that local content considerations must be taken care of. The separate but complimentary roles of the state and private sector

152 *AbdulKarim Mohammed*

and the terms of engagement should be clearly spelt out in all agreements and contracts.

Securing all the above would require extra vigilance that only government (of which parliament is the second arm) can guarantee. Shrouded in secrecy under the pretext of confidentiality, bad contracts are often kept out of reach of the public and rich nations are robbed of their dues. Thus, *contract transparency* is needed to engender the watchdog role of civil society. Collaboration with civil society organisations on these issues can enhance the effectiveness of parliaments in delivering on their mandates.

Prior to all engagements (contracts and agreements) every resource-rich nation must ensure that the institutional, legal, regulatory and contractual frameworks are capable of addressing the needs and potential challenges that the petroleum sector presents. It is only with such an existing framework that effective monitoring of operations, which is the second stage of the value chain, can occur. The monitoring function is crucial in ensuring compliance with contractual clauses as well as international standards of operations. Though this may be the assigned role of a parliamentary committee(s), in-depth technical knowledge is required to undertake good monitoring. As such, committees charged with that responsibility would require the support of a technically competent team or body. In addition to any other committees that may be assigned, the monitoring function falls within the purview of the mines and energy, finance, and environment committees of parliament.

Revenue derived from petroleum resources tends to be the foremost attraction and focus of most resource-rich nations and their citizens. This is because, for both government and private actors, discovery of petroleum portends an opportunity for reaping big money, either by fair or foul means. Accounts abound on how state and private actors have colluded to rip off resource-rich nations. Big money begets big corruption. Thus the collection and utilisation of petroleum revenues more often than not is the focus of both parliamentary and non-parliamentary interrogations. It is by no means an accident that the global transparency framework, Extractive Industries Transparency Initiative (EITI) has revenue collection and utilization as the target on its radar. Though a commendable effort, the challenges posed by the sector are such that connoisseurs are seeking the extension of the initiative across the entire value chain as there are antecedents to what revenue accrues to nations. A bad revenue-sharing arrangement in a contract means that a nation can expect to receive only the crumbs of its petroleum resources. The issue of capital flight can become a serious challenge. On matters of transparency, the central role of a public account committee comes to the fore.

Being the primary function of the finance and mines and energy committees, the choice of fiscal terms is very important in ensuring optimum benefits to a nation. Such terms must be decided in advance with the general frame legislated into law. The law provides clear guidelines on which institution is mandated to collect the revenues and spells out the spending/saving ratios. The procedure for budgeting petroleum revenues must be thought through based on national development priorities. As a best practice, petroleum revenues into the budget must be ring-fenced and tied to specific and identifiable development projects for better tracking. To further the course of transparency, nations are better off when EITI is legislated and legislators mainstreamed in the process.

Having collected the revenues, the challenge that arises is how to transform it into development projects, the so-called lasting benefits to citizens. The bane of many a resource-rich nation is that with big oil money governments become overambitious and embark on grandiose projects most of which end up as white elephants. Without a clear economic policy, a revenue savings and expenditure framework, as well as a transparent redistribution mechanism, there is a strong temptation and tendency to use petrodollars to prop up a nation's currency. Higher currency value makes imports cheaper and local products uncompetitive in price terms, thereby exports from other sectors suffer. With the promise of oil money, governments also tend to go on a borrowing spree, ending up with high debts, over-concentrate on the petroleum sector, and invest less in alternative production. The consequence is the crowding out and collapse of other productive sectors such as agriculture and manufacturing, a phenomenon known as the 'Dutch Disease'. In such an environment, corruption can become a real canker giving rise to increased inequality and resultant poverty.

The panacea for these challenges, as can be deduced from the facts so far, is to get the revenue and expenditure/savings framework right. Then, a strong oversight by parliament through key committees such as the finance, mines and energy, public accounts, employment and social welfare, environment, government assurance, local government and rural development committees, and other sector specific committees depending on what funds are being expended on, will provide the system with the necessary checks and balances. This will ensure that procurement practices are transparent and expenditure at the local level provides value for money.

Oil in itself is not a curse, but what a nation does with it can make it so or otherwise, and there are a number of good examples across the world to confirm this. Obviously, parliaments have a central role to play.

18 Conclusions

Andrew Imlach

Since this book does not seek to compare or assess objectively the parliamentary reforms it describes, and since these reforms are taking place in countries with significantly different traditions, levels of development and parliamentary systems, the advances recounted in the preceding chapters are not a blueprint for the reform of democratic governance in any one country in Africa or elsewhere. But they are much more than a simple collection of descriptions designed, in the philosophy of the parliamentary strengthening programming of the Commonwealth Parliamentary Association (CPA), the World Bank Institute (WBI) and the Parliamentary Centre, to foster understanding and stimulate the consideration of ideas which could be adapted from one parliament to another. The reforms reveal common features which potentially mark them as the next step in entrenching democratic practices in the governance of each of their countries. Their descriptions here constitute a valuable collection of innovations which cast African democratic governance in a whole new and very positive light.

Among the commonalities is that all the reforms are recent, even in terms of the relatively short histories of parliamentary systems in independent Africa, histories of half a century or less. Public meetings of the Ghanaian Public Accounts Committee (PAC), for example, began in 2007 and, while they generated a surge in public interest in and respect for parliament and parliamentarians, their continuation cannot be taken for granted. Nor is there a guarantee that the media will maintain an interest in covering future meetings which should eventually have less dramatic results. The effectiveness of public review lies partly in its power to deter poor government performance and illegal activity, the stuff of media headlines and sound bites such as those which flooded out of the first public hearings. The success of this reform therefore depends not simply on the continued interest of parliamentarians in probing into past accounts, described by Gladstone as a 'dry and repulsive task' when he proposed the establishment of the first public accounts committee in the United Kingdom House of Commons a century and a half ago. It depends also on the maturity of the Ghanaian Parliament's press gallery and media managers in recognizing their responsibility to inform the people about PAC hearings no matter how 'dry and repulsive' they become.

Even the oldest of the reform programmes, Rwanda's transition and recovery programme which started in 1994, is working now on a new Constitution passed only in 2003. Nine years in transition and now seven years in recovery are not long for a nation which went through such a traumatic period after becoming independent in 1962. Similarly, the Nigerian reforms followed a return to democratic governance in 1999 after 17 years of military dictatorship. It was only in 2006 that Nigeria surpassed its previous record of seven years for continuous democratic rule.

We cannot yet gauge therefore whether the reforms outlined in this book will continue to work long enough to become an established part of a parliamentary culture which is well understood and accepted by current and future parliamentarians and parliamentary staff and by their respective societies. We also cannot yet assess whether they will lead to further institutional advances as parliamentarians across Africa strive to increase the contribution they make to the development of their parliaments and their societies. But this is in the tradition of all parliaments where reforms come slowly and follow paths which change with the changing priorities of new parliamentarians facing different challenges. Furthermore, institutional reform should be well considered and this always takes time.

Another of the commonalities is that the bulk of the reforms relate to measures to strengthen parliament's financial scrutiny role. This is not simply because of an understandable interest in finance on the part of the World Bank Institute and the international aid donors who have supported the reforms. This too is in the best tradition of centuries of institutional advances in which parliaments have applied or extended their grip on the government 'purse-strings' to extract from the executive the authority to involve themselves in policy setting and oversight.

Another related commonality is also present: parliaments, their members and their staff still have at best a tenuous grip on their own financial resources and therefore the means to enable them to perform their roles effectively. It may seem petty and self-serving when parliamentarians whose countries face massive problems complain that they need access to vehicles. But this is a reflection not of a desire to acquire a perk of office but of the difficulties in moving around countries which often lack extensive reliable mass transportation networks and whose roads have taken the lives of a tragically high number of parliamentarians and parliamentary officials. How can parliamentarians represent their constituents, or their constituents trust them to do so, if elector and elected cannot meet each other regularly? How can parliamentary committees effectively investigate development projects and weigh the competing opinions of interest groups, the media and government officials if they cannot see projects for themselves – and if the sources of those competing opinions know this only too well?

The availability of resources is a problem even for established parliaments which formally control their own budgets. When governments cut back their ministerial spending, as many are now in response to the global financial crisis, parliaments are expected to follow their lead. Ruling party members of parliament (MPs) on parliamentary management bodies usually ensure they do, even though parliamentary scrutiny and legislative roles actually increase as members must monitor the application and effects of spending cuts and cancelled or reduced policies as well as the effectiveness of continuing policies and spending. Parliaments cannot be seen to be continuing to spend as they wish while voters are experiencing reduced services and higher taxes. Even in the most experienced democratic societies, public opinion can be a negative as well as a positive factor in parliamentary performance and reform.

The fourth commonality is international involvement, especially by aid agencies. In the course of the 1990s, intergovernmental agencies and national aid donors began moving into the parliamentary field after decades of dealing almost exclusively with governments. Their arrival brought to parliaments a new and substantial source of funding and often on-site support which have so far been ongoing and have greatly assisted most of the reforms described here. Parliaments strapped for funding have relied on donor support for training, facilities and even vehicles. Donor pressure is also cited as a significant factor in bringing about some of the reforms, or at least as a factor in building local interest in reform. While donor participation has promoted democratic reforms, its presence poses a problem over the longer term. What happens when it ends? If donor interest moves away from parliaments or away from individual countries, will parliaments be able to fill the void from national revenues?

It is lamentable that it took so long for the international community to recognize that parliaments are as important to governance in Africa and elsewhere as they are to governance in donor countries. But their arrival did have a benefit in addition to facilitating prolonged periods of reform in individual countries: it also caused a number of parliamentary strengthening organizations, such as the CPA and the WBI, to marshal the expertise and experience of parliamentarians and parliamentary officials to draft guidelines for parliamentary reform such as the Benchmarks for Democratic Legislatures developed by the CPA with the WBI, the United Nations Development Programme and others. The international guidelines were originally intended to help donors evaluate the worth of projects proposed by parliaments or by their governments or societies, or even by donor agencies themselves which realized that parliaments needed to improve but lacked the expertise to determine how. But they are also assisting reform-minded parliamentarians to identify changes and to convince colleagues and the parliamentary and governmental establishments to support reform. This has been the case not just in developing assemblies but also in well-established parliaments which have continued certain longstanding practices without realizing that they have not kept pace with new practices, such as Uganda's Parliamentary Budget Office.

Aspects of the African reforms which have emerged through either local adaptation of imported procedures or the creation of new processes may eventually find their way into the Benchmarks and other global guidelines. The role of Rwanda's parliamentary discipline committee in assessing the effectiveness of its Senate and Chamber of Deputies in meeting their constitutional obligations and the Rwandan innovations in the separation of powers among not just the three arms of government (parliament, the executive and the judiciary) but also among the political parties are both innovations which could find application or adaptation in other countries. The Tanzanian decision to move to equal parliamentary representation between the genders by 2020 is another. Uganda's Budget Office, based on the American congressional budget office, is already being used as a model for greater parliamentary involvement in the budget-formulation process than had been the tradition for Westminster-style democracies.

This last reform raises serious constitutional and political issues that parliaments and governments will have to resolve. In the parliamentary tradition, budget formulation is a role strictly prescribed as the right of the elected executive and the full contents of a budget are still formally kept secret (sometimes even from other ministers) until the budget is read in parliament, with the reasons for secrecy being well known and respected. However, parliament's responsibility simply to pass a budget leaves it open to the criticism that it is too passive and subservient a role if parliament is to be seen by the public – and by its own members – as being "relevant". If parliament, particularly in a minority- or coalition-government position, starts to rival the elected executive in determining spending and therefore policy, it could jeopardize current concepts of accountability and responsibility. The executive and parliament could blame each other for spending decisions, ineffective trade-offs and inconsistencies, with voters left confused as to who did what. This is arguably a weakness for which there is ample evidence in the American congressional system. It will then fall to further parliamentary reforms to clarify roles and responsibilities, and parliaments such as Uganda's will undoubtedly be in the forefront of these reforms.

The presence of important local adaptations is perhaps the most important commonality in the reforms. African democratic governance has a long history of transplanted processes. Commonwealth African countries continued the parliamentary systems left from the British colonial period, including in many cases direct references to Westminster practices and precedents in their standing orders. They may have adopted presidential systems modelled on the United States or France; but their parliaments operated along Westminster lines. Other African nations adopted French, American or other countries' systems. Many then followed the lead of the old Soviet Union into one-party governance which suited traditions which did not include the concept of opposition.

The latest reforms reflect broader thinking as assemblies have examined processes in several parliaments, including those in developing and newly developed countries. Some, such as the Uganda Budget Office and the African Parliamentarians Network Against Corruption, have developed their own solutions which have been exported beyond Africa. And among the reforms are many other innovations that merit wider attention. The fact that they are occurring in countries which are developing in economic and social terms makes it more difficult for reforms to be resisted in other developing democracies which can no longer dismiss changes such as holding public accounts committee hearings – and other committees for that matter – in public as developments for which their societies and their media are not ready. At a CPA–WBI videoconference in 2001, it was seriously argued by senior members from one of the countries covered in this book that committees could not meet in public because journalists would not understand the issues or the parliamentary processes and so their flawed reports would mislead people and damage democracy. The Ghanaian PAC's initiative to brief journalists in advance provides an answer to any minister who still tries to argue that journalists should be barred from meetings because they won't understand. At a CPA parliamentary seminar in 2004 in Yaoundé, Cameroonian parliamentarians were visibly shocked to hear about processes and facilities they lacked which were readily available and actively used not in developed Parliaments in Australia, Canada or the United Kingdom but in Kenya, Uganda and Ghana. It is much harder to resist a reform initiative if something similar is already in place in a country which is geographically and economically similar.

Among the innovative reforms is the formal and extensive consultation process for parliamentarians in Benin to be briefed, including by civil society groups, before they question ministers on their budgets. While this may have developed as an alternative to holding committee meetings in public, it is nonetheless an idea that could be attractive to other parliaments, especially those which lack research staff in their parliamentary libraries, committee offices or party rooms. Zambia's establishment of a parliamentary office to draft private members' bills for MPs and the provision of chamber debating time for such backbench legislative initiatives are positive measures many other parliaments, in Africa and elsewhere, could adapt to give members an opportunity to promote the passage of laws that governments do not want or have not considered to be priorities.

Also of significance is the extent to which all of the contributors recognize the need to do more. Parliamentary reform is not a one-off: no parliament, not even the oldest, stands still. None of the well-developed parliaments in countries as diverse as India, Trinidad and Sri Lanka operate the same today as they did a decade ago. African experience in parliamentary reform is shared to encourage others to embark on similar programmes and at the same time to promote the idea that ongoing reform is an established part of the parliamentary process. This is part of the process of deepening the understanding of and the commitment to democratic governance in Africa.

Undoubtedly the most extensive reform programme in Africa today began in earnest after most of this book was written. The people of Kenya in August 2010 voted in a referendum for a new constitution which, among many other things, will establish an elected presidential system of government, add a Senate to parliament, provide for parliamentary oversight of presidential appointments including ministers (who will no longer be elected MPs) and set up 47 new elected governments and assemblies to provide a second level of democratic governance at the county level. This is expected to produce a similar governance structure to the states and provinces of federations. More than 50 bills have to be passed by parliament to implement these and other reforms, all of them in addition to the normal workload of both parliament and the executive.

These monumental changes were made because of the unexpected and uncharacteristic violent reaction to the December 2007 parliamentary and presidential elections. And it is only part of the change as many reforms were made by opposing parliamentarians who seized control of the situation by converting unrest in the streets into action in the parliament.

H. E. Hon. Kalonzo Musyoka, MP, Vice-President of Kenya, summed up the situation in the following words written after the referendum for the CPA journal *The Parliamentarian*.

> We have lived, nay suffered, under the pre-independence constitution negotiated in England with colonial influence. Subsequent alterations by post-independence leaders weakened our institutions and slowed down the uptake of democratic values and advancement of our society.
>
> The post-election violence of early 2008 breathed new life into our search for strong governance institutions built on durable values. Several reform institutions were created by the Kenyan National Assembly and it is that impetus that culminated in the new constitution.
>
> After 2008, the price of poor governance and weak institutions became too clear and dear; it was one we could not bear any longer. Our structural deficiencies had to go; we needed to breathe life into our democracy; change instantly became the Number One item on our national to-do list.

The current Kenyan governance revolution and the reforms which some African parliaments are implementing may not be a blueprint for others in the continent or elsewhere. But they clearly constitute an inspiration and a motivation for all parliaments.

Afterword
Parliamentary reform in Africa?
What are the lessons learnt?
What are the next steps?

Shantayanan Devarajan and Tijan Sallah

The narratives presented in this book are a testament to how, despite the sometimes very challenging context, leadership, foresight and coalition-building within parliament can result in the enhancement of citizen welfare by strengthening the incentives public policy-makers face to pursue a 'good governance' agenda. Parliament is a critical component in the governance processes as, at least in theory if not always in practice, it is the instrument via which citizens' interests are represented in public policymaking. If parliament can exercise effective oversight of the executive and be held to account by citizens, then the prospects for improved governance will be enhanced.

More specifically, the narratives presented in this book can be used to draw two specific conclusions. First, that, despite the significant socio-economic and political constraints they face, the dynamics of change are, broadly, moving towards more accountability (of parliament to citizens) and more oversight (of the executive by parliament). The second, interrelated, point is that this process has occurred, to a large extent, due to the efforts of individual (micro-level) leadership initiatives. While, in many cases, the resources donor organizations have provided have been critical (recall the case of training the media to cover the first public hearing of Ghana's Public Accounts Committee (PAC)) the instigation of reform has been a bottom-up (from members of parliament (MPs) to the public sector at large) rather than a top-down (donors providing resources irrespective of micro-level incentives) process.

This broad trend is therefore, a testament to the importance and centrality of incentives in fostering stronger mechanisms in the fight against corruption and its debilitating effects on socio-economic development. By altering, in some cases in very small ways, the institutional context (increased transparency, development of oversight committees) individual/groups of MPs have been able to alter the dynamics of the political economy of public policymaking in a manner that, at least on the margins, promotes the welfare of citizens. While the magnitudinal impact of these changes is not always large, the case studies in this book clearly suggest that a focus on governance reform can generate real change even if it is not accompanied by a dramatic alteration in the macro-environment of a polity.

Several interrelated factors are critical in securing good governance reforms, namely: (1) leadership, (2) coalition-building, and (3) the ability to secure sustainable institutional reform. Furthermore all three factors have to be tailored to take into account the broader institutional and socio-economic context in which parliamentary reform is taking place. By briefly examining each one of these factors in turn it becomes possible to uncover the logic behind the trend of improved governance that is, slowly and by no means uniformly, altering the governance dynamic in sub-Saharan Africa.

The broader context

The choices agents (such as reforming MPs) make and whether these choices are going to improve good governance by strengthening parliament, is critically dependent on conditioning their actions on the broader context in which they are operating. Not taking into account how contextual factors may alter the constraints as well as the opportunities they face can be a critical factor in determining the success of the reform process instigated by MPs or parliament as a whole. For example, as the chapter on the establishment of the Ethiopian PAC illustrates, attempts to weaken the institutional role of parliament, in order to limit the powers of the opposition, precipitated a political crisis. This crisis was only partly ameliorated when parliamentary reforms were instigated providing new accountability mechanisms (including the establishment of the PAC). Thus, paradoxically, parliamentary oversight was enhanced because the outgoing parliament miscalculated the magnitude of the opposition its attempts to weaken the institution of parliament would generate.

The role of leadership

Context may provide the opportunities and constraints actors face but without individual initiative the ability to seize opportunities to improve good governance will never be realized. (Good) leadership is an elusive quality but can be conceptualized, in terms of its value added, as the ability of a 'policy entrepreneur' to instigate changes which result in a sustainable improvement in outcomes (such as good governance due to parliamentary reforms). As one of the most democratic and stable countries in Africa, Ghana's political context was potentially able to sustain good governance reforms that would increase institutional transparency and social accountability. However, it was only the efforts of the Chair of the PAC to hold inquiries open to the public which resulted in the committee's work being taken more seriously – an outcome which ensured the return of misappropriated public monies to the state as well as creating incentives for public authorities to be more careful in the future, lest their mismanagement and inefficiencies are detected by the PAC and transmitted, via the media, to the general public.

Coalition-building

A context that provides a willing and able policy entrepreneur with the opportunity to engender policy change is an essential prerequisite for facilitating good governance reforms. However, another critical factor which is essential in ensuring the success of this process is the existence of willing partners to support the reform process. Parliament itself may be a forum/conduit for such a reform-minded coalition to emerge. For example, in the post-genocide era Rwanda's Parliament acted as a catalyst for enhancing political and social stability. This was because its cross-societal representation increased its legitimacy amongst different societal stakeholders. As a consequence, it was able to provide a basis for the generation/implementation of national reconciliation mechanisms.

Sustained institutional reform?

Changing institutions, whether these are formal (committees in parliament) or informal (how MPs interact amongst themselves) is, ordinarily, a slow moving process. Given, that much of the Africa region has experienced an institutional nexus which has been plagued by corruption, patrimonialism and the emergence of, more often than not, non-democratic 'strong-men' means that the 'institutional context' is a very challenging one. It is, therefore, always important to distinguish between change occurring on the margin and the status quo. Small incremental reforms which improve good governance over time, and can, therefore, have a critical cumulative impact are not always identified as significant improvements at the moment of activation. This lack of dramatic change has resulted in some pessimists concluding that the chronic problems of poor governance that plague the region are insurmountable and that small incremental reforms will have little impact in altering this dynamic. They argue that these reforms will eventually be undermined by vested interests that have a stake in perpetuating corruption and rent-seeking.

However, this conclusion does not take into account the fact that, despite the chronic problems and challenges faced by the region, on the margins the story is a much more optimistic one. As all the case studies in this book have shown, while institutional reform has sometimes been limited due to resistance and/or a lack of resources, in the end these sometimes small and limited reforms have resulted in sustainable improvements in governance. For example, despite attempts by the executive to prevent its foundation, and continued budgetary constraints, the establishment of Uganda's Parliamentary Budget Office has resulted in increased oversight and accountability, of the executive, to Parliament and more broadly to citizens.

Conclusion

Sub-Saharan Africa is a place of great diversity; it is facing significant challenges in promoting good governance. Despite these perennial challenges and problems the changes made on the margin, while by no means uniform, are broadly in the right direction. That is, while many parliaments in the region remain weak and/or under resourced they are increasingly enacting reforms that are making their oversight of the executive and/or their accountability to voters more effective. Thus parliaments in the region are increasingly playing a more prominent role in ensuring that the dynamics of change are in the direction of better governance even if much remains to be done.

Index

Page numbers in **Bold** represent figures

For Product Safety Concerns and Information please contact our EU
representative GPSR@taylorandfrancis.com
Taylor & Francis Verlag GmbH, Kaufingerstraße 24, 80331 München, Germany

www.ingramcontent.com/pod-product-compliance
Lightning Source LLC
Chambersburg PA
CBHW050446280326
41932CB00013BA/2266